INSIGHTS
Understanding Yourself and Others

Carolyn Marie Mamchur

Occasional papers/23
OISE Press/The Ontario Institute for Studies in Education

The Ontario Institute for Studies in Education has three prime functions: to conduct programs of graduate study in education, to undertake research in education, and to assist in the implementation of the findings of educational studies. The Institute is a college chartered by an Act of the Ontario Legislature in 1965. It is affiliated with the University of Toronto for graduate studies purposes.

The publications program of the Institute has been established to make available information and materials arising from studies in education, to foster the spirit of critical inquiry, and to provide a forum for the exchange of ideas about education. The opinions expressed should be viewed as those of the contributors.

©The Ontario Institute for Studies in Education 1984
252 Bloor Street West, Toronto, Ontario M5S 1V6

Canadian Cataloguing in Publication Data

Mamchur, Carolyn Marie, 1943-
Insights : understanding yourself and others

(Occasional papers ; 23)
Co-published by Ontario Institute for Studies in
Education.
ISBN 0-7744-0269-5

1. Typology (Psychology). 2. Personality.
3. Self-evaluation. 4. Jung, C. G. (Carl Gustav),
1875-1961. I. Ontario Institute for Studies in
Education. II. Title. III. Series: Occasional papers
(Ontario Institute for Studies in Education) ; 23.

BF697.M35 1984   155.2'64   C84-098458-8

ISBN 0-7744-0269-5   Printed in Canada
2 3 4 5 UTP 88 78 68 58

Dedicated to Gordon Lawrence
who, with loving wisdom,
introduced me to the world of typology
and to my mother,
Josephine Thompson,
who, with love and wisdom,
introduced me to the world

Contents

Preface   /vii

Acknowledgments   /viii

1/Run Jung Run — A Typology Primer   /1

The introductory chapter defines psychological type, its implications for the reader, and the best way to use the book according to the individual's own preferred function.

"Practical Psychology"   /1
A Word of Warning   /2
Psychological Type: A Closer Look   /3
A Closer Look at Function Preferences   /10
Extraverted — Introverted Orientation and Type Development   /20
Interface: Coming to Terms with the Environment   /22
Psychological Type: A Brief Summary   /26
What's Next   /29

2/Seeing Is Believing   /31

Chapter 2 focusses on the sensing type and uses both a specific descriptor of what it actually means to prefer sensation and a series of photographs to illuminate the Jungian descriptors of extraversion, introversion, sensation, intuition, feeling, thinking, judging, and perceiving.

Those Intuitives!   /31
A Brief Review   /32
What Is It? What Is It For?   /34
  Extraversion   /34
  Introversion   /35
  Sensing   /37

iv

Intuition /38
Thinking /40
Feeling /42
Judging /44
Perceiving /44
At Last, The Photos /49
  Extraversion /50
  Introversion /56
  Sensing /62
  Intuition /68
  Thinking /74
  Feeling /80
  Judging /86
  Perceiving /92

3/In Other Words   /99

Chapter 3 sees the world through the intuitive's point of view. Each archetype is present to explain, through painting, biography, literature, and photographs, the perspective of the intuitive type.

The Archetype /99
Television /100
Works of Art /101
Literature /112
  Autobiography /112
  Fiction /122
Identifying Types: A Quiz /124
Pure Pleasure /129
  Carousel /130
  Softly /136
  Shared Moments /139

4/A Rose Is a Rose Is a Rose   /146

Chapter 4 deals with the feeling type and describes psychological type through the looking glass of various human misadventures. Situations drawn from actual life experiences are presented in dialogue format.

Ice Fishing /146
"The World of Communication" — An Introvert Talks with an Extravert /150
"What Is It? What Could It Be?" — Sensing and Intuition Try to Understand
  One Another /159
"Please Understand Me" — A Thinking Type Interacts with Several Feeling
  Types /166

"The Dominant Functions in Disharmony" — Judging versus Perceiving /175
How Much Is Enough? /183

5/So What?   /187

This chapter defines psychological type in the clear, factual, analytical format preferred by thinking types. Included in this section is a questionnaire developed by the author whereby readers can assess their own psychological type preferences.

Seven Questions /187
1. Who Am I? /187
   Determining Your Own Type Using the Instant Insight Inventory (I.I.I.) /187
2. How Many Are Like Me? /194
3. How Can I Have My Type Tested? /195
4. Can Type Explain What Motivates Me? /195
5. Does Type Ever Change? /197
6. What Good Does Knowing This Do? /201
   Self-Development /201
   Career Choice /202
   Business /206
   Marriage /209
   School /210
7. Can Type Preference Be Observed? /211

6/in The End, It's Up to You   /218

Appendix: AORO   /223

References   /231

Preface

Workshops, workshops, workshops. Part of my job is to conduct workshops. Teachers attend the workshops to find out about teaching and learning styles; various business and professional groups attend the workshops to learn about career choice options and effective teaming; young almost married couples, middle-years, happily married couples, and almost no longer married couples come to explore mutual understanding or misunderstanding and communication processes.

The workshops vary in focus and audience, but always they centre around the concepts of personality functioning described by the Swiss psychiatrist Carl Gustav Jung as his theory of psychological types. Often, at the conclusion of the workshop, appear the faithful few or the confused few who wish to "find out more." This book is for them. It is for the person having little or no background in psychology in general or Jung's analytical psychology in particular who wants to become familiar with psychological types.

It is for the layman who wants to know the meaning and implications to the self of those terms coined by Jung that have come to be common phrases in everyday conversation. *Extraversion. Introversion. Intuitive.* What exactly do they mean? And what do they mean for each individual reader? Because it is the nature of my particular Jungian type to be very practical, this book is more than a source of definition and clarification. It becomes an exploration in the values of typology for the individual. It explores personal identity, communication and empathy skills, career choice options, advantages to business and professional groups. But most important, it discusses the full potential of the human spirit.

Acknowledgments

I wish to thank my dear friend Jack Wasserman for his careful editing. A brilliant organizer and analyser, he reconstructed Chapter 5 as only an intuitive thinking type could do. I also wish to thank James Lisitza, for allowing me to use his fine photographs for this work, and Sally Parks, for her suggestions from the point of view of a Jungian analyst. A special thanks to my daughter, Mickey, for her good common sense advice and for the wonderful magic particular to the sensing perceiving type. And to Kevin, my loving partner, who kept busy in the garage throwing great pots all the while. And finally, I must acknowledge my debt to Isabel Briggs Myers without whose lifetime dedication to translating Carl Jung's theory of type into observable everyday behaviors, none of this book would have been possible. Her final work, *Gifts Differing*, was a constant source of information and inspiration in editing *Insights*, particularly in rewriting the chapter on Sensation.

Credits

Photographs between pages 49-97 and pages 131-144 by James Lisitza. Cartoons on pages 7, 8, 24, 25, 30, 98, 145, 186 by John Crossen. Cartoons on page 128 by Dennis Smith.

P. 104. Etching by John Leech, from John Leech, *Pictures of Life and Character* from the Collection of W. Punch (London: Bradbury Agnew & Co., 1863).

P. 105. "The Thinker" by Auguste Rodin. Courtesy of The Cleveland Museum of Art, Gift of Ralph King.

P. 106. "Luncheon on the Grass" by Edouard Manet. Courtesy of Musée d'Orsay, Galerie du Jeu de Paume, Paris.

P. 107. "Portrait of Mrs. Stuart Merrill" by Jean Delville, from Robert L. Delevoy, *Symbolists and Symbolism* (New York: Rizzoli International Publications Inc., 1978).

P. 108. "Portrait of Clemenceau" by Edouard Manet. Courtesy of Museum of Impressionism, The Louvre, Paris.

P. 109. "Si son de otro linage" by Francisco José de Goya. Courtesy of British Museum, London.

P. 110. "Portrait of Antonin Proust" by Edouard Manet. Courtesy of The Toledo Museum of Art, Toledo, Ohio.

P. 111. "The Tipsy Woman" by Edouard Manet. Collection of Mr. and Mrs. Arthur Sachs.

1/Run Jung Run –
A Typology Primer

"Practical Psychology"

Communication. Empathy. Self-understanding. Many a philosopher and poet have offered the world a key to these coveted skills which make life so much better for those lucky ones who possess and use them.

Carl Jung was the first to analyse the temperaments of men and women in a way which would systematically enable people to better understand themselves and their loved ones or associates. His method has become known as a study of psychological type and gives order to the apparently limitless variations in human individuality. He examined the various orientations the conscious mind might take towards the world and found that two predominated, that of extraversion (an outward moving, action-oriented attitude) and that of introversion (an inward looking, reflective-oriented attitude). Having made this classification, Jung pursued even further his lifelong goal, "namely, to penetrate into the secret of the personality." (Jung, 1965, p. 206).

Consequently, in addition to the orientation differences of Extraversion and Introversion, Jung recognized different functions to explain the manner in which individuals typically process experience. He maintained that individuals prefer to perceive through either their senses or their intuition; and prefer to make judgments through either their thinking or feeling process. Although all four functions are present in every individual, one is dominant or most favored; one is auxiliary and ranks as the second most used function; the third is a less developed function, less often exercised, and demanding more energy to use; and the fourth is a person's inferior function. The inferior function is the most tyrannical and immature function and is the weak spot in a person's ability to perform whatever task he endeavors to do.

Although the dominant, auxiliary, and inferior functions seem to establish themselves very early in childhood and continue throughout adulthood, they are in a dynamic state and can change in degree both

1

with the situation and with maturity. Ideally, with maturity comes the ability to use whatever function the situation demands. Indeed, it is a natural need of the adult to develop into a more whole being. The inferior function is not only repressed, it is undeveloped. For this reason adults experience this urge to develop it.

Adolescents, on the other hand, need a sense of identity, of who they are. They need to feel secure in this stage of development, experiencing a sense of acceptance at what is their natural preference.

This frame of reference, or schematic approach to understanding motive, behavior, and point of view, should not be considered from a fixed standpoint. No one person stays statically in one category, being all introvert, for example. *The classification merely explains basic tendencies, or preferences, and in so doing gives insight to any interaction.* Accepted in this way, a knowledge of typology is a most useful tool for any mate, parent, teacher — anyone wanting or needing to understand any other human being, or himself. In Jung's words:

> The classification of individuals means nothing at all. It is only the instrumentality, for what I call "practical psychology," used to explain, for instance, the husband to a wife, or vice versa. They are also useful in understanding one's own prejudices.
>
> (Jung, 1964, p. 61)

A Word of Warning

Don't chop off that leg!

At a 1981 conference on the use of the study of psychological types, Scott Golden, President of the Application of Psychological Types (APT), gave a keynote address, the imagery and message of which have not left me. He told the story of Procrusteus, a giant in Greek Mythology, who would invite unsuspecting travelers to spend the night in his home and would then forcibly fit them to his iron bed. If the guests were too large for his bed, Procrusteus would chop off their extremities. If they were too small, he would stretch them out. Either way he invariably killed his guests by forcibly subordinating their individual differences to a system.

It is important that users of the typological system do not chop off a leg to make the person fit the system. Because, after all, any system, any typology, is an abstraction from reality. There is not, nor could there be, any person who was purely one type. Due to personal experience every individual is an exception to the rule in some way. "Conformity is one side of a man, uniqueness is the other. Classification does not explain the individual psyche. Nevertheless, an understanding of psychological types opens the way to a better understanding of human psychology in general." (Jung, 1974, p. 516)

Psychological Type: A Closer Look

In examining psychological type, it is fundamental to understand that Jung considered the various "types" occurring in human nature to be almost instinctive.

> The individual self is a portion or segment or representative of something present in all living creatures, an exponent of the specific mode of psychological behavior, which varies from species to species and is inborn in each of its members. The inborn mode of acting has long since been known as *instinct*, and for the inborn mode of psychic apprehension I have proposed the term *archetype*. (Jung, 1965, p. 376)

Such words as natural, instinctive, automatic, help to clarify the notion of typology. It is obvious that at times some folks are extraverted (outward moving, action-oriented), or deal best in the outer world of people and things, and at other times are introverted (inward looking, reflective-oriented), preferring to deal quietly with ideas inside their own heads. However, one attitude is more natural, more instinctive, more automatic than the other. That one is a typological preference. Jung is responsible for coining the terms *extravert* and *introvert*. In observing his two close friends and fellow psychiatrists, Freud and Adler, Jung became aware that each used an essentially distinctive approach to psychoanalysis.

Freud's approach was very external in orientation, focussing the analysis *outward*, towards the people and events in the patient's past and present environment. This outward focussing of attention Jung labelled as *extraverted*.

Adler, in contrast to Freud, approached psychoanalysis in a more reflective, subjective way. He focussed attention *inward*, examining the personal ideas within his patient's mind. This inward focussing of attention Jung called *introverted*.

In addition to these basic tendencies to direct attention in an extraverted or an introverted manner, Jung observed a common pattern of perceiving and of making judgments. These he called the FUNCTIONS of psychological types.

It is sometimes useful to think of the functions as a large Z pattern.

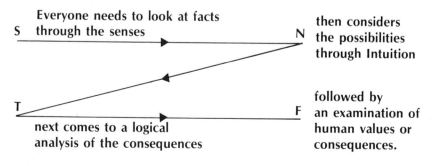

Everyone needs to look at facts
S **through the senses** → N
then considers the possibilities through Intuition

T → F
next comes to a logical analysis of the consequences
followed by an examination of human values or consequences.

These four functions (sensing, intuition, thinking, feeling) all coexist, but one is most preferred and one is least preferred by each of us.

Those who prefer the perceptive function of sensing develop acute powers of observation and awareness. They enjoy dealing with details, with facts, with present realities. As they develop, sensing types rely more on experience than on theory, trust customary ways of doing things, move cautiously from the known to the unknown, and develop a very sound, practical attitude to life, often referred to as "common sense."

Intuitive types, on the other hand, rely on inspiration more than direct experience. They pass quickly over details, see in flashes of insight and work on hunches. Just as the eye teaches the mind of the sensing types, the mind teaches the eye of the intuitive.

Once a person has accumulated data, either through intuition or sensing, then a judgment must be made on that data. Two functions exist, also, for making decisions. These are feeling and thinking. Both are rational processes, insists Jung, and must be accepted as such. The thinking type makes decisions by a logical analysis of the facts. When used in a mature and positive manner, this is an objective, impartial process dedicated to fair play and justice. The feeling type, on the other hand, uses a more personal, subjective process to make decisions. Harmony and compassion guide the feeling type in the development of values and standards. Decisions are then made according to these values and standards.

Myers, whose work in applying and extending the concepts of Jungian type has been widely accepted, felt that it would be most useful to distinguish among individuals according to one further criterion, derived from the two pairs of Functions. Whether a person is an extravert or an introvert, she must *deal* with her environment, her everyday world. How are we most comfortable facing that world? What is our interactive facet, our INTERFACE?

Myers (1962) found that a fourth area of preference exists in each personality, one that favors either Perception or Judging (Decision-making) as a way of coping with its environment. This has important implications for what we *see* when we look at a person interacting with the world around him. When we observe someone who is more comfortable focussing his energies, coming to conclusions, gaining control over events, someone who does not easily tolerate uncertainty or ambiguity, we are looking at a decision-making or Judging (J) type. The person with a Judging Interface seems to aim for *singularity*, a world of resolution and certainty. The Judging type seems to want a structured life, to work well according to a schedule, to appreciate usable systems.

When, on the other hand, we observe someone who is more interested in taking in data, weighing impressions, more concerned with understanding events than controlling them, someone who is uncomfortable with fixed patterns or structures, we are looking at a Perceiving (P) type.

The person with a Perceiving Interface seems to aim for *plurality*, a world of adaptation and change. The Perceptive type seems to want a more flexible life-style, with the freedom to respond to impulse.

Judging types do not judge others (as the name unhappily seems to imply), but rather work best, feel more comfortable in, and use most often, their preferred interface of decision-making. In Judging, their preferred *function* may be either Thinking (T) or Feeling (F). As Judging types are outcome-centred, so Perceiving types are process-centred. They are not more perceptive than Judging types (again as the name may imply), but rather work best and use most often their preferred process of Perception, whether through Sensing (S) or Intuition (N).

Typology might be figuratively imagined like this:

(E) EXTRAVERT	ORIENTATION	INTROVERT (I)
(S) Sensing **(N)** or Intuition	Perceiving Functions	Sensing **(S)** or Intuition **(N)**
(T) Thinking **(F)** or Feeling	Judging Functions	Thinking **(T)** or Feeling **(F)**
(J) Judging **(P)** or Perceiving	Interface	Judging **(J)** or Perceiving **(P)**

One of the difficulties encountered in learning Jungian terms is that many are familiar words to most readers. What is not familiar is the meaning Jung attached to them, his particular usage of the terms. Everyone has a personal interpretation of what Jung meant by his terms, extravert and introvert: "Extravert means gregarious. To be an introvert implies shyness." Not exactly! Sensing? "Oh, I know. It means to 'just know' — as in 'I *sense* this thing.'" Unfortunately, that is the opposite of Jung's meaning. To "sense," in this popular usage of the word, means to *intuit*. To "sense," as Jung uses the word in his typology, means quite literally to *take in with the senses*. The difficulty extends in varying degree to the other five Jungian descriptors: Intuition, Thinking, Feeling, Judging, Perceiving. Readers would therefore do well, as they move through this book, to lay aside their everyday understanding of these terms and to allow the Jungian meanings gradually to take root.

It may be helpful, for a while, to include a new set of terms to accompany the traditional Jungian descriptors.

ACTION	for	EXTRAVERSION
REFLECTION	for	INTROVERSION
REALIST	for	SENSING TYPE
INTUITOR	for	INTUITIVE TYPE
ANALYSER	for	THINKING TYPE
HUMANIZER	for	FEELING TYPE
GOAL-CENTRED	for	JUDGING
PROCESS-ORIENTED	for	PERCEIVING

A Closer Look at Extraverted, Introverted Orientation

Extraversion: *"Bam!" "Kapow!" "Sokko!"*
(Action)   Batman

"I love to DO things, not sit around thinking about them all day."

"Sure I make mistakes, but I can always try again."

"Sometimes I find out just how much I know about something AS I talk about it. I really surprise myself."

"I love being in the limelight."

"It's pretty easy to talk about most things."

"I just naturally trust people."

"I like to check things out with other people, to see how they are doing it."

"I learn by doing."

"I like crowds, small ones, big ones, people just interest me."

"People give me energy."

"My strongest memories are about things that happened to me, and people they happened with."

"I don't mind interruptions."

"I get bored fairly easily."

"I can do several things at a time."

"Apples taste better when they're shared between good friends. Let's buy a dozen."

If you are an extravert, you might be thinking. . . .

"Hey, I'm beginning to understand this typology stuff, I think I'm an extravert, I just can't keep still. . . ."

The Extravert doesn't mind interruptions

Introversion: *"I never found the companion that was so companionable*
(Reflection)   *as solitude."*

Thoreau

"I just have to think about it first."

"Give me a minute, please."

"I'll just listen."

"You can't just blindly trust everyone and everything."

"I KNOW how I want to do it."

"I have had the same two close friends most of my life."

"I just don't discuss certain things with anyone."

"I need a quiet space in which to concentrate."

"I must admit, in the end, a girl is her own best friend."

"I'll think it over tonight, we'll talk in the morning."

"I love to go on long walks by myself."

"If the crowd is big enough I can get lost in it."

"I like to do one thing at a time."

"I can usually concentrate pretty well."

"I hate making speeches."

"The library is one of my favorite places."

"I'd rather do it on my own."

"My favorite memories are the thoughts that ran through my mind during childhood; how pure, how sweet, those thoughts."

"I'll just sit here, munch on my apple, and mull that thought over in my mind."

If you are an introvert, you might be thinking. . . .

"I am considering these ideas on typology, I may just find them useful in understanding myself."

The Introvert tells very few people his innermost thoughts

The essential difference between the extraverted and introverted attitude is direction of focus. Extraverts clearly focus their attention and energies outward on the environment of people and things. This focussing affects the way extraverts act, learn, play, work, relate, all they do.

Extraverts are basically action-oriented. They like to do things. They enjoy especially doing things with other people. Interaction is an activity they are naturally very good at.

Introverts, in contrast, are basically reflection-oriented, needing to think about things, to mull them over, play with them, examine and understand them, before they discuss them or try to "do" them. If an introvert chooses to share conversation or activities, it is usually with a close friend, or with someone who shares a common bond or interest.

Another essentially extraverted trait is a basic trust of the environment. This trust is rarely experienced by the introvert. In addition to this innate trust of others (one that does not necessarily have to be earned), extraverts operate from an external source of motivation. As a consequence, it is not uncommon to find extraverts discussing private affairs with or asking advice from people not too close to them.

If an introvert is inadvertently included in that conversation it can be very upsetting for her. Introverts trust an inner sense of motivation and values. It is not only unnecessary to "check things out" with others, it is often considered (by the introvert) to be threatening. Another view the introvert may take of such behavior is that the extravert is weak, wishy-washy, a Charlie Brown, agreeing with every person with whom he discusses an issue.

Although misconceptions occur from both points of view, it is most common for the introvert to be misunderstood. This may result from the fact that extraverts outnumber introverts four to one (Myers, 1980, p. 54), and it may be further amplified by the fact that introverts never show their best qualities. They reserve their strengths for their favorite processes — inside their heads and hearts. Consequently an introvert is often misunderstood or underestimated. "What you see is what you get" is not true for the introvert. It decidedly pays to look deeper. There is often a treasure chest of ideas or feelings waiting to be discovered and appreciated — but not forced to surface.

Too many an extraverted parent is exasperated by what appears to be a shy, withdrawn, or stubborn child. In reality the child may be reflective, selective, loyal, and adhering to a deep internal set of principles. Seen in this light the child should be appreciated and encouraged, not pushed to "get out more," "liven up," "do it the way others do."

If a child is forced, at an early age, to submit to basic type changes, he may not only never reach his fullest potential by taking advantage of his strengths, but he may become confused and ill. Jung felt this forced type change to be a cause of much later life-neurosis.

A Closer Look at Function Preferences

Sensing: *"Common Sense is Genius in its Working Clothes"*
(Realist)   Emerson

"I usually get the facts straight."

"Yes, I guess I do have a lot of common sense."

"Sure, I'm practical."

"Let's get a more realistic picture of what's going on."

"Could you give me a more specific example?"

"What's this good for?"

"Can't we do it now?"

"I have a memory like an elephant."

"Seeing is believing."

"It's the little things that count."

"Let's stick to the facts."

"A picture is worth a thousand words."

"When I think of an apple I think red, juicy, sweet."

If you are a sensing type, you might be thinking. . . .

"I've almost got it. Just give me one more specific example, a practical one please.

Everyone has a pretty clear idea of the way the sensing function works. It is obvious that the body and mind process data by means of the senses. We understand an apple exists by tasting its sweetness, feeling its juiciness, smelling its fruitiness, seeing its red roundness, hearing its crunchiness. Our eyes, fingers, lips, tongue, ears tell us "appleness." These are the facts about apple, the details, the precise data banks for information that feed our senses.

Most people in the Western cultures of civilization rely most heavily, most naturally, on the sensing function to process information. Only one-quarter prefer the less specific, more unconscious approach called intuition. What few people realize are the ramifications of having preferences.

Those people preferring the sensing function are practical, realistic, fun-loving individuals. Although I am an intuitive type, I can speak fairly easily about the sensing types because two of my favorite people, my daughter and my mother, are sensing types. Often we learn to appreciate our different, or "shadow" function by living with them. Sensing types trust, appreciate, and put energy into the here and now. Because response to the senses is immediate, their focus in life is immediate. To say to a sensing type (especially a young person), "Let's work on this project because the skills we learn will come in handy some day," is a useless motivation. The sensing type wants to see an immediate practical reason for what is being done.

This attention to the present tense, this impatience with delay, and this fine-tuned sensitivity to factual detail makes the sensing type a persuasive person. He can argue very powerfully to support an idea or, more particularly, a plan of action he wants executed. In some instances the sensing type's lack of focus on the overall pattern, on future consequences, and on possible hidden agendas may lead to lack of wisdom or narrowmindedness. However, it is more often the case that the sensing type is renowned for possessing a good deal of "common sense." This common sense grows quite naturally from a practical nature paying close attention to factual detail.

The sensing type is blessed with a love of the everyday things in life. It does not take grandiose schemes or magical dreams of future or long-term ecstasy to please or stimulate a sensing type (as it may her intuitive neighbor). Instead, the sensing type seeks pleasure in the specifics of now. She loves a sunset, not for the dreams of pots of gold or romantic memories it evokes, but for the splendor of color her eyes explore.

This enjoyment of what's happening right now may frustrate the sensing type if he, for example, is attending a movie which forces him to miss a football game on the TV. The videotape recorder must have been invented for the sensing type — not so that he could be a selective viewer, but so that his senses could enjoy each moment of each day. "You fill up my senses," sings John Denver, and the sensing type only smiles. The intuitive wonders what that exactly means, but he has five or six possible explanations.

As the intuitive trusts his ability to speculate on the future, the sensing type relies on immediate data and on past experience to guide his actions. If past experience has been bad, it will be difficult to persuade a sensing type to risk a similar adventure.

This assimilation of past experience as an essential part of the person's data bank has important implications for how a sensing type learns. Whether the learning occurs as math in a classroom, running a lathe in a sawmill, or sewing a dress in the home, the sensing type will learn best if she moves slowly from the known to the unknown. New skills must be acquired one step at a time, with plenty of practice time before new learning is tackled. The learning will go better if stages are clear, reasons for doing things a specific way are apparent, and there is a practical consequence involved.

Intuition: *"Ah, but a man's reach should exceed his grasp, or what's a*
(Intuitor) *heaven for?"*

Browning

"Ideas just seem to come to me."

"I'm pretty good at reading between the lines."

"Well, it's just a hunch, but I really think. . . ."

"It's a sixth sense I have, I just seem to know."

"One thing just seems to make me think of another."

"There sure are a lot of possibilities here."

"If I were Prime Minister. . . ."

"My sister always says I can figure out the theory of relativity but can't count the number of people at the dinner table."

"When I think about an apple I think of my grandmother's garden, Adam and Eve, the movie, *The Three Faces of Eve*, the clown at the circus, the day my little boy fell off his tricycle. . . ."

If you are intuitive, you might be thinking. . . .

"I've got the picture, let's get on with this section. Let's look at the implications."

Intuition is a way of perceiving, of bringing information to the mind and spirit. It is a process used as often by men as by women. It is a process preferred by about one-quarter of the population of North America.

As popular myth would have it, intuition is a quality possessed by the magic, the creative, the prophetic peoples of the world. And surely, science shows that those people possessing creative abilities, or "ESP" powers, are indeed very intuitive. And perhaps we can call this magic. But magic not in the sense of the mysterious, the non-definable, the "other" world of witches and fortunetellers.

Intuition is, according to Jung, a function of perception, a function as natural as its corollary function, sensing. As it is easy to imagine certain folks bringing in information consciously through the senses, so should it be acceptable to imagine them perceiving by means of insight. It is an unconscious gathering of facts.

Both sensing and intuition exist in and affect all of us. But one is stronger, more obvious, more natural in each of us. Surely the person preferring the intuitive function, or having intuition as a dominant pattern, uses the conscious senses in learning about the world. But if an intuitive person is closely questioned about how he knows things, it becomes apparent that the intuitive is quite shaky when it comes to details involved. A good example of this is what an intuitive will remember about a story or novel he has read. The intuitive will not be too sure who the characters were, what they looked like, where they lived. But he enjoys speculating on why the character chose to live there, or what will happen next, or what might have happened if circumstances had been different.

The intuitive in the family is not the person to ask if you need a telephone number or a specific date as to someone's birthday or anniversary. A very intuitive person is so timeless or so future-oriented that she may be hard-pressed to give not only the day of the week, but the month and the year she is living in. However, if someone is needed to guess what the boss really thinks, or what a boyfriend might do, or what the poem is all about, the family or classroom intuitive is asked.

This very process of asking of one another those things which each does best seems a natural way in which families strengthen the functions each family member has at birth. It is important to strengthen the dominant and auxiliary functions.

Although it is natural to appreciate, use, and thereby strengthen favorite functions in one another, it is also natural for family members to misunderstand one another's differences. A mother, for example, who definitely prefers the sensing function can become extremely exasperated with her intuitive teenage son who constantly gets mixed up in directions, getting lost even in familiar territory. The mother tends not to believe that the son is seriously trying, thinking instead he is just careless or silly. The same mother who enjoys the advantages of having her son sensitive to small nuances or mood changes in the rest of the family, of seeming somehow just "to know" what will happen at the family picnic, and how to prepare for it, of being able to handle many projects and ideas at one time, that same mother often refuses to accept the fact that her son does not enjoy fixing the car, does truly forget to mail the letter she has asked him to post, or that he finds day-dreaming a meaningful and pleasurable experience.

The same "plus" and "minus" perceptions of the intuitive's habits occur at school. Teachers are very pleased with the intuitive's ability to learn to read, and to be interested in books in general. And indeed, the intuitive, being a lover of the abstract, the symbolic, finds the translation of symbols into words a very natural process. Many intuitive children come to school knowing how to read. Fantasies, myths, legends, occupy their interest. Such children move easily and happily through the various phases of language arts and literature programs. As students who naturally enjoy complicated procedures, they learn new material fairly rapidly. Indeed, the intuitive student often amazes a sensing teacher with her ability to "catch on" to such subjects as Latin, physics, and geometry in such a "flash."

What doesn't thrill the teacher quite so much is that the intuitive student also gets bored or restless quite easily, especially when doing repetitive tasks or when learning subject matter involving a close examination of facts. The intuitive is inclined to skip over the facts, sometimes getting them wrong, in his enthusiasm for getting on with the task, or with its implications.

Enthusiasm is a good word to use when talking about the intuitive. Such a student may become very excited about a project or idea, may stir up enthusiasm in others, and then, long before the task is completed, may drop it, feeling perhaps disinterested, but more likely feeling more excited about a new project which has captured his imagination. Teachers often interpret such behavior as wishy-washy, flighty, uncontrolled, non-committed. Actually the intuitive is often very committed — but to many projects, and to the planning, instigating, and dreaming up of ideas. Only if the idea continues to challenge will the intuitive continue to feel a need to stay "on task." The key here is to allow the intuitive a challenging role, and to allow the intuitive to conduct many tasks simultaneously.

Another interesting dichotomy exists in the attitude both parents and teachers feel towards the young person who is a strong intuitive. Intuition is strongly associated with imagination, insight, creativity. Adults enjoy this facet in the child, finding it at times charming, stimulating, fascinating. Adults feel a sense of pride at the child's creative product, be it a thought, a painting, a poem. But often the adult is not so happy with the process. The whole creative act is a very individualistic one, involving others only in rather superficial ways. Others may spark or encourage the process, but only the individual can, herself, create. It is unique, it belongs with the creator, and above all, is evaluated by the creator. This internal locus of evaluation, according to such experts on creativity as Paul Torrence and Carl Rogers, is the most fundamental condition of creativity. This same internal locus of evaluation, this saying to parent or teacher, "But I must do it my way, it is ultimately myself whom I must satisfy," is a most unpopular characteristic in the eyes of adults.

It is important, first of all, to help the intuitive strengthen and prize his intuitive preference. Only then will he be free to develop the weaker, sensing function. This can be done by prizing the qualities the intuitive does possess, by recognizing weaknesses to be what they are — those things that one is not naturally inclined or able to do — and by guiding the young person with sensitivity in those weak areas. It helps to recognize that the child is not choosing to be "flighty," "careless," "lazy," "disrespectful" — but is independent, future-oriented, and has difficulty paying attention to details, or staying "on task."

Understanding of typology gives clearer insight to individual differences and behaviors. It provides opportunity for greater understanding, communication, and prizing. Such understanding and need for development is not limited to adult–child relationships.

Once "type" is understood, the intuitive wife, for example, no longer can, in good conscience, criticize her sensing husband as being too "slow," "careful," "pernickety" or "common." The wife should appreciate that the husband is careful and painstaking, is down-to-earth, and has great common sense. These assets are wonderful for money management and for decision-making. The name calling, the frustration and misunderstanding and hard feelings occur when the mates demand that each be what the other naturally is.

Neither mate can truly believe the other *naturally* operates in such a different manner. Often they blame caring, or lack of caring, as the culprit. "If you cared about me, you wouldn't. . . ." The true culprit is lack of understanding. If the opposite or "shadow" side of the mate is seen for what it is — a part of the temperament that doesn't work too well — the husband and wife would not only feel better about the relationship, about little causes of irritation, but the causes would lessen. "Dream on, wife," smiles the husband, "and I'll keep our feet on the ground." And she does, and he does, and differences are complemented.

Not only can differences be complemented, but each person can grow when pressure is released. Maturity is achieved when the person can use whatever function the situation demands. The least favored or shadow function can never be used with the ease, the lack of energy, the natural instinctive manner, as can the dominant. It can, however, like the left-handed to the right-handed person, be mighty useful!

Thinking: *"Justice is Truth in Action"*
(Analyser)   Disraeli

"Look at the facts, will you?"

"The only logical conclusion. . . ."

"If that is true, then. . . ."

"From the evidence presented, I can only deduce that. . . ."

"I must do the fair, the just thing."

"I understand how you feel, but. . . ."

"It has nothing to do with how I feel, that's the way things are."

"Let's examine this a little more."

"I want to make this very clear to you at the beginning."

"This is the truth about eating apples."

If you are a thinking type, this may be running through your mind. . . .

"I could sure say this with more objectivity and brevity."

It has been common to most nations of the world to view the male as a strong, unemotional, logical, analytical type. The qualities of compassion and "emotionalism" have been attributed to the woman. This latter description has carried with it the connotation of flightiness, silliness, an element not to be trusted in times of crisis. Clearly it has been the tradition of many peoples to honor the cool-headed, detached, rational decision-making process of the male. This process, fairly familiar to us all, describes the thinking function. And, indeed, 60 percent of North Americans tested out to be thinking types are males; 40 percent are females. The reverse is true of the feeling function (60 percent are women, 40 percent are men).

Isabel Myers' latest research suggests that since the sixties this statistic has begun to change. A balance is starting to emerge. Thinking types would enjoy analysing why this would be so. Do people's type preferences change as does custom? The cultural revolution of the sixties made feelings and the open expression of feelings more popular. Women's roles also changed, as women refused to be considered ineffective and unreliable. Will the change be permanent? Will this attitudinal change be reflected in people's type preferences in the year 2000? Is preference, then, a product of environment?

Or could it be that men and women were always more "balanced" in this function and only now are they feeling free and safe enough to admit it? The Myers Briggs Type Indicator (MBTI) is a forced-answer, self-report questionnaire. In times when to rely on feeling implied a feminine quality, it is quite likely that a male would be reluctant to answer certain questions truthfully. Even his subconscious could affect his answering. Our responses are always affected by our phenomenal field, and societal expectations are influential. This fact could be true for all aspects of the MBTI. It is only more clearly so in the thinking/feeling category.

It seems to me (and this may be purely a feeling type's conviction) that on the larger scale of things, from a "whole society" point of view, we prefer the thinking function; but on a personal level, feeling is favored.

And we are sometimes uncomfortable with the fact that individuals cannot switch from one to the other with more ease.

The clearest example I can find of a preference for the thinking function on a large scale is our judicial system. It is designed to work in a logical, objective, analytical manner. Initially laws may be set according to the feeling function, that is, according to the value system of the community. But when laws are broken the thinking function is set into motion. Great pains are taken to insure that an objective rather than a subjective decision be made.

Let me give a specific example. Imagine that a murder has been committed in Vancouver. Hypothesize, too, that capital punishment has been re-established in Canadian courts. I am subpoenaed to serve on the jury at the trial of the accused. My personal value system, which I *think* about very carefully, tells me that I do not believe in capital punishment. This, then, is a feeling decision. It is essential to realize that the feeling function does not lack thought — it is a rational process, involving the thinking process. The essential difference is that the decision, for a feeling type, is based on a *value system*; and for a thinking type, is based on a logical *analysis of facts*.

Because my value system does not allow me to look at the facts objectively, I would be excused from jury duty. The system wants jurors to base decisions on an objective look at the facts presented. I would have to find the accused not guilty simply because my value system disallows capital punishment. This does not fit into the thinking judicial system of "true-false," of *objective truth*.

The problem with objective truth, of course, is that the facts may be incorrect or the logic faulty. Feeling types (not good at this logic) are especially suspicious of clinical analysis. They feel more confident in basing decisions on what is clearly *valuable* to them, rather than what might be "truth."

In law, business, science and government, thinking is clearly preferred. These comprise the "large issues" of society and have been basically run by men. However, in personal matters, in marriage, teaching, counselling, and nursing, in basic human relating, feelings are preferred. Here the social arts are more valued than executive ability. Here tact is often more useful than "objective truth." Here the use and easy expression of emotion is important. No one wants a mate, a priest, a teacher to be curt, business-like, critical. Rather, they want the tenderness, appreciate the empathy, the regard for harmony so characteristic of feeling types.

Ideally, both can be used, at times, by everyone. Different situations demand the use of different functions. However, it is natural for one to be the preferred function. And this preference will affect our interactions with other people, our choices of jobs, our attitudes towards all important decisions made by us and those affecting our lives.

Feeling: *"Heroism feels and never reasons and therefore is always right"*
(Humanizer)   Emerson

> "But these are just the facts — what about the effects they have on other people?"
>
> "The truth is seldom black or white."
>
> "I just can't seem to challenge him on that."
>
> "I hate conflict."
>
> "Give me harmony any time."
>
> "What is really important to me is. . . ."
>
> "It's easy for me to say how I feel."
>
> "Computers seem to frighten me."
>
> "Sometimes I just can't seem to explain myself logically."
>
> "When I'm not clear about my beliefs. I just can't make a decision."
>
> "I don't know what to do — neither thing seems right."
>
> "This is what I care about when deciding to share my apple."

If you are a feeling type, you might be thinking. . . .

> "I think I'll learn this, it seems it will be useful for communication skills."

Feeling is the rational process of making decisions based on one's value system. The process breaks down, or becomes difficult, when values are unclear or are in conflict. Let's return to the case of the feeling person declining to serve on a jury because of a disbelief in capital punishment. That person may equally feel that it is not right to incarcerate a person for life. Yet to commit murder is wrong and society must be protected from such wrong-doings. The value system is in conflict. There is no easy solution. If the prisoner is convicted, the law provides three possible sentences: death, life imprisonment, a sentence with possible parole. The feeling type's value system rejects the first two possibilities as inhumane; the third as unfair to society. Such states of conflict and therefore indecision can cause the feeling type to be so distressed as to become ill.

On the other hand, when a feeling type is sure of his convictions, he is a confident decision-maker. He may ignore or undervalue logical analysis altogether.

One of the nicest side "benefits" of the feeling preference is the ability to understand how others are feeling. This empathic ability is appreciated by all types. It is difficult for the thinkers to understand its source. And it is natural for them to want to *understand* or analyse, rather than simply accept it.

An explanation I often offer is the feeling type's need of harmony. This need is so powerful it causes this type to tune in very carefully to the needs and attitudes of others. The indifference or critical approach often offered by thinking types can lead to conflict. Feeling types are so uncomfortable with conflict they not only avoid the critical, impersonal mode, but they employ a personal, compassionate attitude towards others. Group harmony usually depends on the "people" skills offered by feeling types.

Convince a thinking type that tuning into other people's feelings or into her own value system is a logical thing to do — necessary, for example, in the pursuit of peaceful living, or fair play, or justice — and the thinking type will take measures to develop her shadow function. It becomes part of the logical analysis of data, part of the skills developed by a rational, reasonable being. But even when a thinking type becomes very skilled at using the feeling function, a person whose dominant preference is feeling will still notice a "coldness" or a "hardness" or a "missing out of the little important things" in the relationship. It is very difficult for a feeling type not to be "hurt" by a thinking type from time to time.

A wonderful example of the different point of view experienced between a thinking and a feeling type is told by Sheldon Kitt in *Folklore of the MBTI (1981)*.

> Last year, I had to take my car to the garage for some repair work and I asked Stella to follow me in her car so that I would have a ride home. It was one of those days when the heavens just opened and spilled water down in torrents. Had there been a Chesapeake waterman around, he would have called that kind of rain a regular frog strangler.
> On our way to the garage, I recognized a neighbor, umbrella in hand, boots on his feet and a slicker tight around his chin. He was trudging through the storm and since he didn't drive a car, due to an earlier equilibrium loss, he had the thumb of his free hand stuck out for his usual hitchhike.
> My T thought process began to weigh the facts and probabilities of the situation. If I pick up my hitchhiking neighbor, I will have to stop my car rapidly. Perhaps this would cause Stella to ram into the back of my car, bringing an accident or possibly even injury. The garage we are heading for is located on a very busy intersection. What happens if my passenger gets hit by my wife's car as he is getting out of mine? In this rain, the visibility is so poor that I will be inviting trouble or possible injury if I stop suddenly and pick up our neighbor. Thus went the logic.
> Needless to say, Stella stopped, picked up our neighbor, and let him out at the busy intersection at which the garage was located. You can

imagine her F reaction when we finally got home. "How could you ignore someone walking in this downpour?" she shouted. "You must now feel terrible for doing such a heartless thing!" "Not I," I replied calmly. "I just saved both your lives and you haven't even bothered to thank me."[1]

Knowledge of typology can help feeling types to use their natural empathic qualities in understanding the thinking person's point of view and thereby be neither too hurt by, nor too demanding of, their mates or friends or bosses or students. It is essential to recognize the difference between lack of emotion and lack of expression of emotion. A thinking person finds it difficult to say what he is feeling. In fact, the need to do so is not clearly evident. In the thinking type's logical attitude, emotions should simply be apparent as a consequence of actions. "Why dwell on them, anyway?" ponders the thinker.

"Why, indeed," answers the feeler. "Because they are the essence of life." In comparison all else is shallow. The essence of the feeling type's preferences can be seen to the extreme in the English Romantic period of the eighteenth century which revolted against the dogma of reason, the mechanized philosophy of the Neoclassic period which claimed, "I think, therefore I am." (Descartes)   Shelley's passionate humanitarianism epitomized the Romantic doctrine of the time: "I feel, therefore I am." (Shaftesbury)

Extraverted–Introverted Orientation and Type Development

The manner in which each person manifests the preferred function in everyday life will depend upon the favorite attitude of each. Extraverts put their attention outward, towards people and things. Their bent on life is objective. Introverts focus their attention inward, towards their inner world of ideas, their bent on life being subjective. Extraverted thinkers, for example, want to criticize or organize their environment; extraverted feeling types are more interested in the helping professions, such as nursing, teaching, the ministry. Concerned with values, they may champion or protest aspects of society (law, government, civil rights). Extraverted sensing types enjoy the environment, or at worst put up with it rather graciously. Generally they are adaptable realists. They work well with things, machines, paint, lumber. Extraverted intuitive types, being enthusiastic and innovative, are interested in changing their environment. They too enjoy

---

1. *Folklore of the MBTI, 1981.* A collection of anecdotal stories available from Association for Psychological Type, Gainesville, Florida. Reproduced by permission.

teaching and nursing; but usually such types leave the field, earn Master's degrees, and return in the hopes of improving their professions.

Introverted intuitives, on the other hand, would be more inclined to write about changing their professions and developing theories. They are driven by an inner vision, and delight in pioneering new ideas. Introverted sensing types also look inward for inspiration. Less interested in change, they concentrate their efforts on being systematic and painstaking. They have keen inner perception but this is usually kept to themselves in work situations. Inner harmony is most valued by the introverted feeling type. Although feelings are seldom expressed, they are deeply felt and motivate the introverted feeling person to work quietly, individually, in any area in which he perceives a need. The key to this person's work is a vocation involving personal values. Introverted thinking types tend to be more analytical and impersonal than other types. They enjoy organizing concepts and ideas, but not people or situations, unless they have to. Relying on the extraverted thinking types to run the world, they concentrate their efforts on figuring it out.

In order for type development to take place in the individual, it is essential that both the perceiving and the judging function be encouraged. One is dominant in each of us, the other is auxiliary; one we extravert with, the other we use in an introverted manner. If either the extraverted or the introverted orientation is checked, or blocked early in life and thwarted in its growth, the chance of full type development is also thwarted.

Herein lies the irony of the situation. It is natural for an individual to develop his auxiliary function if he feels confident in using his favorite, or dominant function. As in every life situation, if one feels confident about oneself, if one's perception is, "I do things well, I trust myself," then risk is not such a frightening thing.

A confident, *extraverted sensing* type, when given the facts, will begin to trust her inner judgment and will begin to make good decisions based on the dominant function, perception. Her inner judgment is auxiliary, and is an introverted process.

If, however, an intuitive parent, for example, gets annoyed at the child's need for facts, for looking closely at details, and pushes a more global "creative" approach to perception, it is unlikely the child will feel confident enough to use either function, particularly the auxiliary function, well.

This "pushing" of young people into an opposite mode of behavior is often most apparent when an extraverted father wishes his introverted son to be more outgoing. Ironically, the best way to help reduce the child's "shyness", "lack of vigor", or "unsociability" is to allow the introverted preference to be accepted and established in order to give a sense of confidence and control to the young person. Only then can he feel safe enough to practice his need — and desire — to be an extravert.

Forcing only makes less likely the very attitudes the parent values. Ironically, too, as the extraverted parent matures he comes to value the introverted tendency more. As we reach our forties, we tend to move towards a valuing and a need to practice our "opposite" preferences more frequently. Unhappily, that appreciation can come too late for the "redirected" child.

Myers (1980) speaks highly in favor of the rewards of good type development.

> The extent to which type is developed affects not only the value of the inborn type but also the value of the inborn intelligence. Within limits, type development can *substitute for intelligence*, because average intelligence, fully utilized through fine type development, will give results far above expectation. However, a serious deficit of type development, especially a deficit in judgment, constitutes a disability for which no amount of intelligence can compensate. In the absence of judgment, there is no assurance that the intelligence will be brought to bear upon the necessary things at the necessary times. (p. 186)

Interface: Coming to Terms with the Environment

One of the keys to successful happy living is the development of the Judgment process in dealing with one's environment. On the other hand, overemphasis on Judgment, to the neglect of Perception, can lead to trouble, even to tragedy. The extremes may perhaps be best understood if we contrast two extravert personalities.

Everyone has experienced within his family or among his acquaintances those individuals possessing ample charm and intelligence, but who somehow just can't seem to make it in the workaday world. They move aimlessly from job to job, never really getting "their act together." Such folks, being unable to make decisions easily, cannot firmly handle difficulties. Often they consider work to be a difficulty, and avoid too deep a commitment to it. They have ready excuses for their "bad luck" on the job market, blaming a host of people and circumstances. What is too painful for them to admit is that it is their own inability to organize their environment, to make decisions, to come to closure on events, which inhibits professional success. What this person has not developed is the Judging process. In all likelihood, the person is an extraverted *perceiving* (EP) type.

The opposite "handicap" can be seen in the extraverted *judging* (EJ) type. If their perceiving process has remained undeveloped, EJ types jump to conclusions so quickly, they may make false or unfair judgments and hasty decisions or bad decisions. The tragedy is that judging extraverts with undeveloped perception may never discover their problem. It is the data-processing function which they lack, the very means to "discover the problem."

Extraverts quite often experience more difficulty in these respects than do introverts. They trust their environment, and so interface with it by using their dominant or most-favored function. If they are Perceiving types, for example, they will "show the world" their dominant Sensing or Intuiting function. Because they feel free thus to lead with their most-favored function, often they will not feel it necessary to develop their second-favored auxiliary function, in this example either Thinking or Feeling, taken from the "rejected" Judging, decision-making realm. This can be a tragedy. It is essential that children and adolescents be encouraged or at least be allowed to develop their dominant functions. For complete type development to take place, however, the individual must learn to trust and use his auxiliary as well.

Introverts are often more fortunate in this respect. Because they have a far lesser trust in their environment, they tend to keep their dominant or most-favored function to themselves, to use in their inner world. Thus, if they are to deal with the outer world at all, they *must* develop their auxiliary function. An introvert who doesn't is painfully withdrawn and uncomfortable in all contacts with the environment.

This intricate relationship between a person's inward (I) or outward (E) orientation and the preferred behavioral process (either a P function or a J function) that person uses in interfacing with his environment will be discussed in greater detail on pages 27 and 28. An individual's interfacing strategy itself, however, is fairly simple to determine by observing how that individual behaves in, and deals with, the environment. A judging type wants a very organized life-style.

Judging: *"The secret of success is constancy to purpose."*
(Goal-Centred)   Disraeli

"I just know the way things should be."

"It is easy to make up my mind."

"I need to decide a thing before I can get on with my life."

"I love agendas."

"I need some structure in my life."

"I need to plan ahead."

"Once I start something I like to finish it."

"It's easy for me to organize my activities. Easy? it's necessary!"

"I seem to get my way quite often, or at least that's what people often say."

"Having a schedule is most helpful."

"It's important to keep time lines."

"I have all the information I need. Let's get *on* with it."

"Product is more important than process."

"The proof is in the pudding."

"I know a good apple when I see it."

If you are a judging type, you might be thinking. . . .

"I know just how I am going to use the ideas in this book."

The Perceiving Type has a carefree kind of attitude

These statements epitomize the judging type's preference for the decision-making function. It doesn't matter whether the judging type prefers feeling or thinking; what matters is that it is easier to make a decision than it is to process data. This makes either feeling or thinking the favorite function for dealing with the environment.

Such a preference mandates that the person live in a regulated organized manner. She enjoys schedules and specific deadlines. She must finish tasks she has begun. She has a secure sense of the way things ought to be and puts energy into bringing events to fruition according to a predetermined plan.

The perceiving type, in contrast, enjoys a more flexible, spontaneous life-style and open-minded focus.

Perceiving: *"Important principles may and must be flexible."*
(Process-Oriented)   Lincoln

"I need more information before I can decide."

"There's got to be more to it than that."

"Being on time is not one of my strong points."

"I hate following a schedule, I'd rather do things as the spirit moves me."

"Not all things are worth finishing."

"Let's keep an open mind here."

"Sometimes I'm like a chameleon, just changing with the situation."

The Judging Type knows the way things ought to be/makes decisions easily/doesn't change mind/duty oriented

"Are you sure all the information is in?"

"Routine bores me."

"You never know what might happen next — isn't it wonderful?"

If you are a perceiving type, you might be thinking. . . .

"Before I decide to use these ideas on typology I'd like to find out just how they affect the classroom dynamic."

The person who could say most of these phrases is a perceiving type. He enjoys most, and uses most naturally, most spontaneously, the perceiving function of intuition or sensation. This preference causes the person to focus attention on processing data. Decisions can and must be put off until enough information has been obtained. Projects may be started and abandoned. Routines steal energy and cause boredom.

The perceiving type's life-style is a more easy-going one than is his judging counterpart's. Although this search for more data, this procrastination, this dislike of routine may at times trouble the perceiving type, he does enjoy many benefits from his preference. He is flexible, open-minded, adapting, understanding.

Psychological Type: A Brief Summary

(E)	EXTRAVERT	ORIENTATION	INTROVERT	(I)
(S)	Sensing or	Perceiving Functions	Sensing or	(S)
(N)	Intuition		Intuition	(N)
(T)	Thinking or	Judging Functions	Thinking or	(T)
(F)	Feeling		Feeling	(F)
(J)	Judging or	Interface	Judging or	(J)
(P)	Perceiving		Perceiving	(P)

Once an individual's overall type has been determined, his dominant and auxiliary functions flow naturally from that overall type. An extravert will interface with his outer world using his *dominant* or most-favored function. (An Extraverted-Sensing-Feeling-Perceiving (ESFP) type, for example, will show most clearly his Sensing function.) Less in evidence will be his *auxiliary* or second-favored function (Feeling, for the same ESFP).

Shows or Extraverts with Dominant Function

(E)	EXTRAVERT	ORIENTATION
(S) (N)	Sensing or Intuition	Perceiving Functions
(T) (F)	Thinking or Feeling	Judging Functions
(J) (P)	Judging or Perceiving	Interface

An introvert, on the other hand, will reserve her *dominant* function for her preferred inner world and will interface with the outer world using her auxiliary function. (An Introverted-Intuitive-Thinking-Judging (INTJ) type, for example, will show most clearly her Thinking function. We must not forget, however, that this is her *auxiliary* function. Being an introvert, she keeps her dominant function of Intuition to herself.)

Shows or Extraverts with Auxiliary Function

ORIENTATION	INTROVERT	(I)
Perceiving Functions	Sensing or Intuition	(S)
		(N)
Judging Functions	Thinking or Feeling	(T)
		(F)
Interface	Judging or Perceiving	(J)
		(P)

(*A Note on the Inferior Function*: An individual's least-favored or inferior function is that which "opposes" his dominant *in its own domain*. (For the ESFP cited above, the inferior function will be Intuition; for the INTJ, it will be Sensing.) The inferior function (as its name implies) tends to intervene when the personality is "under a cloud," and is likely to reveal a negative or even troublesome aspect to the observer as well as to the individual who experiences it. Total type development and maturation will be discussed in Chapter 5, pages 197 to 201.)

A consolidated diagram of typological possibilities, then, might look like this:

(E)	EXTRAVERT	ORIENTATION	INTROVERT	(I)
(S)	Sensing or Intuition	Perceiving Functions	Sensing or Intuition	(S)
(N)				(N)
(T)	Thinking or Feeling	Judging Functions	Thinking or Feeling	(T)
(F)				(F)
(J)	Judging or Perceiving	Interface	Judging or Perceiving	(J)
(P)				(P)

dominant determinants (left)   *dominant determinants* (right)

What's Next

As we have seen, people may use any one of four functions as the dominant process in their lives. And like the people themselves, each of these functions is unique; each is valued; each makes an important contribution. Because each dominant function has its own special focus, each is given a chapter in this book which examines the range of psychological type from that special point of view. Thus the book is organized so as to provide entry points to a study of Jungian psychological types tailored, in turn, to the Sensing, the Intuitive, the Feeling, and the Thinking approach. Implicit in this method of organization is the important notion that no single point of view is sufficient. You, the reader, may wish to move directly to the chapter (as described below) which appeals to your own favorite function. Or (especially if you are an S, a T, or both) you may feel more comfortable taking the chapters in the order in which they appear. It may be that you might wish to return to the chapter representing your favorite function for a second reading. Whatever path you choose, by the time you have finished your journey, I hope that you will have actually experienced each dominant function, with its special point of view.

Chapter 2, "Seeing Is Believing," is designed to inform and please the sensing type. Practical descriptions clarify what it means to prefer each of the different aspects of psychological type. The focus is particularly on the sensing type, showing how sensation interacts with each of the (E, I) orientations (T, F), judging functions and (J. P.) interfaces. The focus of the chapter is a series of photographs representing the eight aspects of psychological type. These were chosen both for their archetypal quality and for their unique beauty which, it is hoped, will delight sensation.

Chapter 3, "In Other Words," is designed to stimulate the imagination of the intuitive. Because the intuitive sees possibilities, hidden meanings, relationships in everything, I have presented a variety of illustrations of psychological type. These illustrations exist everywhere — in dreams, in art, in TV, in biography, in literature, in photography.

Chapter 4, "A Rose Is a Rose Is a Rose," is my favorite chapter. This is natural. The judging process I prefer is feeling. The words just ran as I wrote this section. It felt real. My purpose in writing was a feeling purpose — to help the communication processes of the reader. Feeling types are always more interested in doing something if it is of personal humanistic value. The conversations in Chapter 4 are designed to clarify each aspect of psychological type by looking directly into people's interactions. Types are juxtaposed to illustrate different attitudes and perceptions and the conflicts they sometimes engender.

It was with less ease that I tackled Chapter 5, 'So What?" Designed for the thinking type, it is logical, analytical, objective. I am not. However, espousing the notion that understanding of type allows for better communication, I've put my beliefs to the test. The chapter attempts to ask and answer seven questions which may occur to the thinking type:

1. Who am I?
2. How many are like me?
3. How can I have my type tested?
4. Can type explain what motivates me?
5. Does type ever change?
6. What good does knowing this do?
7. Can type preference be observed?

It is possible that the thinking type would feel more confident and more motivated to read the entire book after having these questions answered.

However, it is also logical that the thinking type read in a sequential pattern. Hopefully, if you are a thinking type, you have enough data to facilitate a sound choice. It was my intent that you do.

And now, wherever, whyever, however, I invite you to continue.

The Sensing Type goes cautiously from the known to the unknown

2/Seeing Is Believing

Those Intuitives!

Writing an explanation that would satisfy the sensing type is a challenge for any writer. When the sensing type gathers information he trusts the written word least of all. Ultimately a REALIST, the sensing person learns through experience, relying on the five senses to tell her directly what is happening at the very moment of its occurrence.

Writing an explanation that would satisfy the sensing type is a particular challenge for this writer. Because intuition is my favorite function, sensation is my least favoured preference. Operating in this is most difficult for me. Every time I came upon a way to write this chapter, I would ask my daughter, a sensing type, what she thought of it. "Well, it would sure take an intuitive to think of that!" And away I would retreat to my drawing board. At last I had it! "Sensing types coined the phrase, 'a picture is worth a thousand words,' wouldn't you think?" I asked her.

"Probably."

"And sensing types love pleasure?"

"You got it," my little joie de vivre child smiled to herself.

"Well, look at these!" I showed her a collection of photographs taken by a dear friend, a photographer, who had lived and worked in Saskatchewan, my home province.

"Oh, these are dynamite." She started to examine the pictures.

"This is how I'm going to explain psychological preference for the sensing types." I was proud. She looked at me in absolute disbelief. "Mom, these are pictures of grain elevators!" She shook her head and walked away mumbling something about "intuitives."

I had to admit I was stretching it. To the sensing type the thing is the thing. A grain elevator is a grain elevator. And an extravert may be an extravert, but what does that mean? The notion of extraversion is an abstract concept. To make concrete this abstraction, I have linked it with a specific thing — a picture of a grain elevator. The different preferences are expressed in the different views of this concrete object. Luckily my friend, James, had taken such a variety of photographs so that the essence of each psychological preference was easily represented by them. A pattern emerged, yet there was uniqueness in each photograph because that is the natural and wonderful complexity of existence. Thus it is with people. Each is unique, just as each also demonstrates an archetypal preference.

My daughter was not yet convinced. "Remember," she warned, "James is the same type you are — these are pretty intuitive-feeling type pictures. If a sensing took a picture of a grain elevator it would be a lot more straightforward. Look at this — it's only a shadow of a grain elevator. It's a picture of a girl. And look at this — where's the grain elevator in this picture?"

I pointed at a window in the picture. "See this?" And there, through the window, was — you guessed it — a grain elevator.

"Well," she said, "sensing types may have fun with this — and the pictures are beautiful. . . . but, you'd better make sure your sensing readers are clear about the terms first. And understand what good knowing this stuff will do.

"I'll try," I promised. And I am.

A Brief Review

In our study of psychological types, four basic aspects of human behavior can be seen.

Aspect One: ORIENTATION (how the person directs energy).

Aspect Two: PERCEIVING FUNCTION (how the person processes information).

Aspect Three: JUDGING FUNCTION (how the person makes decisions).

Aspect Four: INTERFACE (how the person interacts with the environment).

For each of these aspects, personal preferences tend to settle between two extremes:

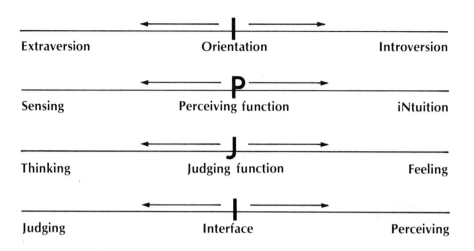

Extraversion	Orientation	Introversion
Sensing	Perceiving function	iNtuition
Thinking	Judging function	Feeling
Judging	Interface	Perceiving

(You will notice that the first letter of each word stands for that word, except in the case of intuition. N is used for intuition because I has already been used to denote introversion.) Thus eight different preferences, eight different modes of behavior can be seen. A preference is just that. Nearly every person will, at one time or another, operate in each of the eight modes of this system, but he will not be equally comfortable, feel equally natural, in each. For each aspect, he will prefer *one* mode of behavior.

By choosing one of the two possible preferences for each of the four behavioral aspects, we get sixteen possible personality types:

ISTJ	ISFJ ·	INFJ	INTJ
ISTP	ISFP	INFP	INTP
ESTP	ESFP	ENFP	ENTP
ESTJ	ESFJ	ENFJ	ENTJ

If you wish to determine your own preference before continuing in this chapter, I suggest you turn to page 188 and take the Instant Insight Inventory. Those folks with these combinations of letters use *Sensing* as their favorite, or dominant function.

ESTP

ESFP

ISTJ

ISFJ

What Is It? What Is It For?

A detailed description of what it means to prefer the sensing function. . . .

Extraversion

A Description

Extraversion is an outward focussing of energy. This orientation to life can result in a variety of behavioral patterns:
- Extraverts put energy into motion.
- They crave action.
- They demand a breadth of understanding.
- They easily focus attention on the people and things in their surroundings.
- They like to share their ideas.
- They enjoy participation in a variety of activities.
- They have a practised ability to exchange information.
- They often think things through while talking about them.
- They sometimes interrupt others in their eagerness to contribute their ideas.

On the Job

If you share your work with an extravert, you may see these effects of her preference in the following ways:

Extraverts

● Like variety and action.

● Tend to be faster; dislike complicated procedures.

● Are often good at greeting people.

● Are often impatient with long slow jobs.

● Are interested in the results of their job, in getting it done and in how other people do it.

● Often don't mind the interruption of answering the telephone.

● Often act quickly, sometimes without thinking.

● Like to have people around.

● Usually communicate freely.

Myers, 1974, p. 8

Getting Along with Others

If you are an extravert's mate, or friend, or business partner, it might be helpful to both of you to remember that his reality is this:

- he requires a lot of your time and attention.
- he naturally seeks a variety of activities.
- he enjoys sharing many friends.
- he often speaks without thinking.
- he can express ideas, even feelings, easily.
- he is fairly easy to understand.
- he is quite accessible.
- he understands life by living it.

Characteristics

If you have scored E on the Instant Insights Inventory, these words might describe you:

ACTIVE	CONFIDENT
PRAGMATIC	EXPANSIVE
VERBAL	OBJECTIVE
SOCIABLE	IMPULSIVE

——————— ✳ ———————

Introversion

A Description

Introversion is an inward focussing of energy. This orientation to life may result in a variety of behavioral patterns:

- Introverts get energy from motion.
- They crave reflection time.
- They demand a depth of understanding.
- They prefer to focus attention on the inner world of ideas.
- They are careful listeners.
- They like to concentrate on a few select tasks at a time.
- Their attitude is reserved and questioning.
- They carefully consider an idea before discussing it or making a decision concerning it.
- They have a practical ability to be inconspicuous, sitting back, observing and reflecting.

On the Job

If you share your work with an introvert, you may see these effects of his preference as follows:

Introverts

- Like quiet for concentration.
- Tend to be careful with details; dislike sweeping statements.
- Have trouble remembering names and faces.
- Tend not to mind working on one project for a long time without interruption.
- Are interested in the idea behind their jobs.
- Dislike telephone intrusions and interruptions.
- Like to think a lot before they act, sometimes without acting.
- Work contentedly alone.
- Have some problems communicating.

Myers, 1974, p. 8

Getting Along with Others

If you are an introvert's mate, or friend, or business partner, it might be helpful to both of you to remember that her reality is this:

— she requires a lot of time alone.
— she dislikes interruptions.
— she can't be pressured into talking about an issue until she is ready.
— she may find it difficult to express her emotions in an open way.
— she is loyal.
— she is intense and passionate, taking life seriously.
— she must understand a thing before she tries it.

Characteristics

If you have scored I on the Instant Insights Inventory, these words might describe you:

REFLECTIVE	OBSERVANT
SERIOUS	INDEPENDENT
QUIET	SUBJECTIVE
RESERVED	SELF-DISCIPLINED
INTENSE	

———— ✳ ————

Sensing

A Description

SENSING is a perceiving function which depends directly on the five senses for information. It is independent from the extraverted and introverted orientation. There can be extraverted or introverted sensing types. This orientation to life can result in a variety of behavioral patterns:

— sensing types are realistic.
— they spend a good deal of time in collecting data.
— they have an internal filter for sorting out impractical ideas.
— they need a firm base in experience.
— they are concerned with what is happening in their immediate environments.
— they tend to focus on one thing at a time.
— they crave enjoyment, seeking pleasure in life.
— they are intensely aware of what is happening around them.
— they like to work with tested ideas.
— they are patient with routine detail.
— they enjoy a standard, patterned way of doing things.
— they exceed in common sense.

On the Job

If you share your work place with a sensing type, you can see these effects of his preference:

Sensing Types

● Dislike new problems unless there are standard ways to solve them.

● Like an established way of doing things.

● Enjoy using skills already learned more than learning new ones.

● Work more steadily, with realistic idea of how long it will take.

● Usually reach a conclusion step by step.

● Are patient with routine details.

● Are impatient when the details get complicated.

● Don't often get inspired, and rarely trust the inspiration when they do.

● Seldom make errors of fact.

● Tend to be good at precise work.

Myers, 1974, p. 8

Getting Along with Others

If you are a sensing type's mate, or friend, or business partner, it might be helpful to both of you to remember that his reality is this:

— he will be a pleasure seeker.
— he is keenly aware of and affected by his physical surroundings.
— he likes things to be real, to be definite.
— he is practical, possessing a great deal of good common sense.
— he is imitative, wanting to have what others have.
— he mistrusts vague, abstract ideas, and wants the facts in discussing an issue.
— he dislikes postponements.
— he is essentially a realist, and takes things "as they are."

Characteristics

If you have scored S (Sensing) on the Instant Insights Inventory, these words might describe you:

SPECIFIC   PRACTICAL
OBSERVANT   AWARE
REALISTIC   IMMEDIATE
PLEASURE-SEEKING

If you are both an E (Extravert) and an S (Sensing type), you might see the interaction of these two aspects of psychological types as influencing you in such a way that you are:

— especially practical
— good with your hands
— sociable
— relaxed and confident

If you are both an I (Introvert) and an S (Sensing type), you will be:

— keenly focussed on your environment
— loyal
— painstaking
— patient

———————— ✳ ————————

Intuition

A Description

INTUITION is a perceiving function which is indirect and which works from the unconscious.

This indirect approach makes immediate assumptions about the information it receives from the conscious world of the senses. The mind is the "eye" for the intuitive perceiver. This function is independent of the orientations. There can be extraverted or introverted intuitives. But there cannot be sensing intuitives. The person naturally chooses a preference between the direct or indirect way to perceive. This intuitive orientation to life can result in a variety of behavior patterns:

— they tend to skip quickly over data, going immediately to the possibilities, the consequences, the various associations the data suggests to them.
— they will gladly sacrifice a realistic approach in search of the imaginative, the creative, the symbolic.
— they take things figuratively.
— they are future-oriented, always seeking the potentiality, the possibility behind something.
— they tend to scan their world.
— they crave innovation, change, variety.
— they sometimes seem unaware of their surroundings.
— they enjoy the challenge of the untried, wanting to take an innovative role.
— they easily become bored with routine and tend to make mistakes in or quit jobs that consistently demand tasks being repeated. This is especially true if attention to detail is demanded.
— they are excellent inventors and implementors.

On the Job

If you share your work place with an intuitive type, you might see these effects of her preference:

Intuitive Types

● Like solving new problems.

● Dislike doing the same thing over and over again.

● Enjoy learning a new skill more than using it.

● Work in bursts of energy powered by enthusiasm, with slack periods in between.

● Put two and two together quickly.

● Are impatient with routine details.

● Are patient with complicated situations.

● Follow their inspirations, good or bad.

● Often get their facts a bit wrong.

● Dislike taking time for precision.

Myers, 1974, p. 8.

Getting Along with Others

If you are an intuitive type's mate, or friend, or business partner, it might be helpful to both of you to remember that his reality is this:

— he will crave inspiration, living his life in a cyclic pattern of being inspired and going like a house on fire, to being uninspired and disinterested until inspiration hits again. To put it briefly, he is a "spurter."
— he may seem indifferent to many aspects of his environment, actually he simply doesn't notice a lot of things.
— he hates being pinned down to a definite way of doing things, always seeing new possibilities.
— he can be disarmingly impractical.
— he is often indifferent to conventional notions of success or creature comfort.
— he often changes his mind in mid-stream.
— he is inventive and creative, a great problem solver.

If you scored N (Intuitive) on the Instant Insights Inventory, this chapter does not include specific descriptions of your type. It concentrates primarily on Sensation.

———— ✳ ————

Thinking

A Description

Thinking is a judging function which relies on objective logic as a means of making decisions. It is independent from the orientations and the perceiving functions. There can be any combination of introverted or extraverted, and sensing or intuitive thinking types. (EST, IST, ENT, INT). This preference may result in a variety of behavioral patterns:

— Thinking types value logic.
— They often come across as being impersonal.
— They pursue justice and fairness based on the rules.
— They try to establish objective criteria for making decisions.
— They are negotiators, looking objectively at the evidence.
— They are task-oriented.

— They find it difficult to express personal feelings, especially if they are introverted thinking types.
⊾ They value analysis and clarity.
— They require logical order.
— They perceive the world to be in a true–false relationship.

On the Job

If you share your work place with a thinking type, you may see these effects of her preference:

Thinking Types

● Are relatively unemotional and uninterested in people's feelings.

● May hurt people's feelings without knowing it.

● Like analysis and putting things into logical order. Can get along without harmony.

● Tend to decide impersonally, sometimes ignoring people's wishes.

● Need to be treated fairly.

● Are able to reprimand people or fire them when necessary.

● Tend to relate well only to other thinking types.

● May seem hard-hearted.

Myers, 1974, p. 8

Getting Along with Others

If you are a thinking type's mate, or friend, or business partner, it might be helpful to both of you to remember that her reality is this:

— she may appear cold, suppressing deep emotions.
— she hates, above all, what she considers to be unfair play.
— she needs systems and order in her life.
— she must understand cause-and-effect relationships in order to function.
— she tends to criticize, seeing it as a helpful way to improve life.
— she tends to be more truthful than tactful.

Characteristics

If you have scored T on the Instant Insights Inventory, these words might describe you:

IMPERSONAL   FAIR
LOGICAL   CLEAR
CRITICAL   BUSINESSLIKE
ANALYTICAL   HONEST

If you are an extraverted sensing type who prefers thinking as a judging process, your psychological initials will be EST(P) and you will often be:

— matter-of-fact
— straightforward
— outspoken
— resourceful

If you are an introverted sensing type who prefers thinking as a judging process, your psychological initials will be IST(J) and you might see the interaction of these three aspects of psychological type as influencing you in such a way that you are:

— thorough and effective
— conspicuously patient with detail
— able to experience intense personal reactions to sense impressions.
— sensible and serious

Feeling

A Description

Feeling is a judging function which relies on a rational but subjective weighing of values as a means of making decisions. It is independent from the orientations and perceiving functions, allowing these combinations (ESF, ISF, ENF, INF). Thinking and feeling are bipolar. One is preferred. This preference can result in a variety of behavioral patterns:

— Feeling types rely on personal values.
— They are often warm and personable.
— They pursue harmony in their relationships.
— They develop personal subjective decision-making criteria.
— They care mostly about the principles involved behind issues.
— They express emotions easily, having a natural ability to say the right thing at the right time.
— They require personal warmth and harmony in their lives.
— They see issues in terms of right or wrong.

On the Job

If you share your work place with a feeling type, you may see these effects of his preference:

Feeling Types

- Tend to be very aware of other people and their feelings.
- Enjoy pleasing people, even in unimportant things.
- Like harmony. Efficiency may be badly disturbed by office feuds.
- Often let decisions be influenced by their own or other people's likes and wishes.
- Need occasional praise.
- Dislike telling people unpleasant things.
- Relate well to most people.
- Tend to be sympathetic.

Getting Along with Others

If you are a feeling type's mate, or friend, or business partner, it might be helpful to both of you to remember that her reality is this:

— she needs a harmonious environment, and shies away from conflict situations.
— she does not value criticism.
— she tends to agree with people around her, believing them probably right.
— she finds it difficult to be brief and businesslike.
— she is not always able to express herself in a logical sequential way and may appear (especially to the thinker) to be a rambler.

Characteristics

If you have scored F on the Instant Insights Inventory, these words might describe you:

WARM	SENTIMENTAL
CARING	PEOPLE-ORIENTED
FRIENDLY	AGREEABLE
COMPASSIONATE	

If you are an extraverted sensing type who prefers feeling as a judging process, your psychological initials will be ESF(P) and you will often be:

— tolerant of others and of yourself
— essentially conservative, valuing traditions
— sociable, fun-loving
— charming

If you are an introverted sensing type who prefers feeling as a judging process, your psychological initials will be ISF(J) and you will often be:

— responsible
— loyal
— aware of a deep need to be of service to others
— dedicated

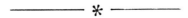

Judging

A Description

Judging is a preference in the way one chooses to interface, or deal with the environment. This interface is an extraverted process which concentrates energy on making decisions. The decisions can be based on thinking or feeling, depending upon the person's judging function. This preference for judgment can cause a variety of behavioral patterns:

— Judging types believe the world should be "a certain way."
— They like things to be settled.
— They have a definite and preferred way of doing things.
— They crave clarity and order in all things.
— They organize their activities according to specific schedules and long-term plans.
— They bring things to closure, liking to finish what they begin.
— They are often high achievers, applying sustained determination to achieve impressive results.
— They have a need to have things settled, decided, resolved, and operating.

On the Job

If you share your work place with a judging type, you can see these effects of her preference:

Judging Types

● Are at their best when they can plan their work and follow the plan.

● Like to get things settled and wrapped up.

● May decide things too quickly.

● May dislike to interrupt the project they are on for a more urgent one.

● May not notice new things that need to be done.

● Want only the essentials needed to get on with a job.

● Tend to be satisfied once they reach a judgment on a thing, situation, or person.

Myers, 1974, p. 8.

Getting Along with Others

If you are a judging type's mate, or friend, or business partner, it might be helpful to both of you to remember that his reality is this:

— he needs to have a plan.
— he may jump to conclusions rather hastily out of his need to have things decided.
— he can often be very opionated.
— he craves resolution, feeling wonderful when things are settled or completed.
— he may appear to be (and sometimes is) inflexible because of this strong tendency to have things "the way they ought to be."
— he is often strong and most reliable.
— he gets the job done.
— he has a deep sense of responsibility.

Characteristics

If you have scored J on the Instant Insights Inventory, these words might describe you:

SYSTEMATIC	DECISIVE
ORDERLY	SUCCESSFUL
INFLEXIBLE	RESPONSIBLE
CLEAR	

If you are a combination of Sensing and Judging -S-J, you might often be:

— a giver, a caretaker, an especially responsible person.

— feeling a deep sense of obligation, of duty.
— conservative, a "saver-of", a traditionalist.
— in need of a specific routine in your life.

If you are an introverted sensing type IS-J, you will use judging (either thinking or feeling) as your extraverted or second favorite process and sensation as your dominant or most favored process. This means that although you choose judging as a way of dealing with the environment, you prefer perception above all processes. Your judging must be developed to prevent an ignoring of the world and an uncommunicative attitude. As an ISFJ, an introverted sensing type with feeling, you might see the interaction of these four aspects of psychological type as influencing you in such a way that you are:

— loyal
— considerate
— concerned about people
— painstaking

As an ISTJ, an introverted sensing type with thinking, you might see yourself being:

— logical
— analytical
— decisive
— thorough

————————— ✳ —————————

Perceiving

A Description

Perceiving is a preference in the way one chooses to inferface or deal with the environment. This interface is an extraverted process which concentrates energy on gathering information. The gathering of information can be done through the senses or the intuition, depending upon the person's preferred perceiving function. This preference for perceiving may result in a variety of behavioral patterns:

— Perceiving types do not have preconceived ideas about how things are, preferring an investigative attitude to things.
— They have a high need for an open, spontaneous life-style.
— They have a zest for experience, tolerating a good deal of ambiguity.
— They need a flexible life-style which does not tie them down and prevent their enjoying the unexpected.
— They may procrastinate in search for more and better information.

— They are excellent at gathering data, emphasizing diagnosis over concluding and resolving. Theirs is a very process-oriented approach.

— They have an exciting sense of curiosity which demands an open door policy to life.

On the Job

If you share your work place with a perceiving type, you may see these effects of his preference:

Perceptive Types

Tend to be good at adapting to changing situations.

Don't mind leaving things open for alterations.

May have trouble making decisions.

May start too many projects and have difficulty in finishing them.

May postpone unpleasant jobs.

Want to know all about a new job.

Tend to be curious and welcome new light on a thing, situation, or person.

Myers, 1974, p. 8

Getting Along with Others

If you are a perceiving type's mate, or friend, or business partner, it might be helpful to both of you to remember that her reality is this:

— she needs flexibility.
— she may put off making decisions.
— she hates being tied down to a schedule.
— she is tolerant, having a live and let live attitude.
— she is curious, finding interest in almost any situation.
— she has a marvellous zest for life.
— she craves the spontaneous, the unexpected.
— achievement is not high on her list of priorities.
— she is usually untidy and relatively disorganized.
— she may be late for things, even when she cares.
— she is non-judgmental, enjoying and accepting people as they are.

Characteristics

If you have scored P on the Instant Insights Inventory, these words might describe you:

TOLERANT   SPONTANEOUS
CURIOUS   FLEXIBLE
OPEN   INDECISIVE
ADAPTABLE   SHALLOW (if commitment is lacking)
UNDERSTANDING

If you are a combination of Sensing and Perceiving, -S-P, you might often be:

— driven by a need to be free, free to do as you wish.
— impulsive, enjoying, giving in to the excitement of the moment.
— charming and cheerful.
— possessing an endurance that allows you to put up with discomforts or deprivation that other types find intolerable.

If you are an extraverted sensing type, ES-P, you will use judging (either thinking or feeling) as your second favorite process. That means that you deal in the world with your sensation. This makes you an active, adaptive, resourceful realist. Craving action, unhindered by preconceived notions, keenly observant, tuned into the present situation, you make an excellent trouble-shooter. Got a crisis? Call in the ES-P!

As an ESFP, an extraverted sensing type with feeling, you often are:

— optimistic
— voluble
— tactful
— gregarious
— lenient
— unpredictable

As an ESTP, an extraverted sensing type with thinking, you often are:

— resourceful
— action-oriented
— accurate
(in straightforward matters)
— reliable
— astute
— excited by danger

At Last, the Photos

The following photographs epitomize each aspect of psychological type as expressed in the different views of the subject, the Saskatchewan grain elevator. There are three photographs, and three accompanying descriptions for each aspect of type. The words most denoting each preference are italicized. Although it is the primary purpose of this book to inform, this section is intended to also delight the reader. Turn the page, please, and feast the senses.

Extraversion

Energy, of sky, of elevators, of children, are captured in the time and space of this first photograph. It represents the *action-oriented* motif, involving alert group *interaction* and awareness of the *environment* so much a part of EXTRAVERSION. In addition, we see emphasized the whole notion of *group expectations, group norm,* and wanting to *please others* so imperative to this outward-looking attitude.

In this image is captured the *easy relating* associated with EXTRAVERSION. *Interaction* is obviously enjoyed by the grain elevator employees. *Interest* is moving *outward* from person to person. The whole picture draws *attention* to the *external* environment of things and people, rather than the internal world of ideas. In looking at the photograph you notice the people, their interaction, the desk, newspaper, the coffee pot, milk cartons, and in the distance, the grain elevator itself, a whole host of *practical things*. You can imagine that what these folks are talking about is less important than that they are *speaking*. This is a typically extraverted point of view.

An early morning sun awakens a Saskatchewan day to reveal a truck, full of grain, and ready for the road. This *outward-moving* vehicle symbolizes the *practical, action-oriented* mode of EXTRAVERSION. *Bold, dynamic, open,* the image *reveals itself* and *welcomes* its *environment.*

Introversion

In contrast to the outward moving, action-oriented elevator scene on page 55 this same subject illustrates the *reflective independence* of the IN-TROVERT. Housing *its own answers,* the building allows the potted geraniums to hint that the introverted type reveals its inner thoughts to a select few. The shaded roof-top room to the left of the image suggests the hemming-in darkness of the sky, suggests *introspection* and *quiet.*

Again, a *quiet independence* is the focus of this image. True to the IN-TROVERTED mode, the tree and the elevators prefer *peaceful meditation* to interaction. Even in the face of a windy environment an *inner strength* and *concentration* pervades. This independent strength is often seen by others as stubbornness or indifference, or as self-isolating. Look again, softly please.

"*Inward-focussing,*" "*moving towards the self,*" "*ideas within ideas*" describe INTROVERSION, describe this picture. Refusing to acknowledge even the wild grain threatening to enter its doors, this building *does not interact* willingly with its environment. *Subjective, private,* it warns intruders not only to refrain from smoking but to refrain from entering. The road is gone, swallowed by grass and weeds, and the buildings stand alone with their own memories.

Sensing

Almost every aspect of the SENSING function presents itself in this image, which both appeals so much to the *senses* of taste, sight, touch, smell, and sound, and which speaks the *practical, common-sense* language of the *here and now*. In the mode of the *factual*, the *detailed*, of *establishing patterns*, lists appear on the blackboard and messages are written on walls, doors, and milk machines. The messages themselves appeal to common SENSE, encouraging the dweller to "insure" to "drink milk" and to "treat customers well." Even the pails are arranged in a *pattern* awaiting *usefulness*. This is a *real* room of the *present*, a no-nonsense room of *sensibility* and *practicality*.

Both the room and the man represent the *realistic, practical* attitude of the SENSING function. The room is organized with a fine regard for *detail* and for objects *immediately useful*. "Phone C. N. Central" at this *precise* time, a cardboard notice reminds us, and one would expect equally *sound advice* from the gentleman clearly *tuned* into the *here* and *now*. Nick's hands are large and open, hands which *work* hard and *feel* warm.

There is no lack of *detail*, of appeal to the *senses* in this third representation of the sensing function. The window affords a brief, bright *view* of earth and sky and elevator. The counter is alive with promised *smell* and *taste*. *Close examination* demands that you notice the love of *design* in checkered curtains, in kitchen tiles, of arrangement in yellow daffodils and waiting turkey. Small *ornaments* adorn window ledge and cupboard shelves. But even more than the love of *detail*, of *design*, is the overall impression of *immediate usefulness* and *practicality* so typical of the well functioning SENSING type.

Intuition

The *spiritual*, the *abstract*, the *symbolic* all belong to the world of the IN-TUITIVE; all are framed within this image. The flowers on the grave stones, the graves themselves, the crucified Christ against a cloudy sky, the grain elevators, symbols of the prairies, all *stand* for something, *suggest*, to each individual, some *special meaning*, linking present to past to *future*. What is meant, or felt, is often *vague* or *shadowy* — but *real* and *powerful*. It sweeps the *imagination* and the *soul*. It goes *beyond reason*, it merely *is* the intuitive.

"The promise of" whispers to the imagination in this image. And suddenly, all at once, the impression is made. Without articulating the details of sky and tree and soil, the wind allows the mind to analyse, synthesize, feel its magic, know it, without understanding. Abstract, symbolic, this photograph captures the essence of. . . .

Passing quickly over details, perhaps even inaccurately, getting a *global impression,* a *synthesis,* of what is *happening* is how one views this picture. Trusting your *hunches,* you *imagine,* the *mind* telling the *eye* just what *might happen* here. True to the INTUITIVE mode, *details* are in the *shadows,* and in a *flash of insight,* like the light, *understanding,* perhaps even *irrational* understanding, occurs. *And the mind,* provoked by the image, may travel from *thought* to *thought,* from *idea* to *idea,* from *image* to *image.* It may move from an empty grain elevator to a night job in a packing plant, to a potential robbery, to a single cell in death row in Utah State Penitentiary.

Thinking

Judgment based on logical analysis of facts epitomizes the THINKING function. And it's exactly what one would expect from this pool elevator agent. Texts on such subjects as "Chemicals," bulletin boards of notices, a myriad of form papers, and file folders of data are close at hand to provide all the *information* needed to function in a *systematic, clinical* manner. The need for *organization* declares itself to an almost ludicrous degree by the three calendars adorning, in succession, the cupboard doors. An additional desk calendar sits below these three, "just in case." As you look into the eyes of this man you might guess he would value *justice* more than *harmony* and you would be better off talking *facts* than *feelings*.

It is important to understand that although the *language* of the THINKING function is that of *cool logic*, emotion is often involved. The feeling "fear" might immediately seize the traveller wishing to short-cut through this yard, a *logical analysis of the facts* would guide the *decision* to "take the long way around."

A *cool head*, a *steady hand*, that's what it takes to be a "straight shooter," whether you are dealing with machines — or people. Again, emotion may be involved in this THINKING function, but the *final decision* is based on *clinical analysis*. The young boys *do not* express a need for *harmony* as they examine this stranger intruding upon their territory. Part of the emotion they may feel might be curiosity or resentment, but in deciding how to react to the photographer one sees a critical scanning, and then it's "a cool head," a steady hand, and on with the game. . . .

Feeling

In contrast to the clinical attitude prevailing in the thinking function, this image represents the overall sense of *harmony* and *values* so crucial to the FEELING function. *Comfort, caring,* a *personal touch* are symbolically expressed by the soft lighting, the clean kitchen, the radio, the many plants. "Sit down and share some fine talk, a cup of tea." And you guess you just might, your hunch being that it would "feel" *ok*. This "feeling" is not a romantic gush of extreme emotion, but rather a comfortable, harmonious approach to living.

Framed in the doorway of this huge elevator walk three men, strong, sure, men of *conviction*, needing one another, valuing *harmony*, giving mutual *support*. These men typify the spirit of the farming community where dedication to *values*, to a love of the land, of *depending* on one's self and one's neighbors, of co-operative, communal living is the common base for many of the major decisions having to be made each day. And in this spirit is typified the essence of the FEELING function.

Wee, sleekit, cow'rin, tim'rous beastie
Oh what panic's in thy breastie!

Robert Burns

Empathy, compassion, for whom? The fox, perhaps killed by the hunter's gun, the farmer's scythe? The chickens, too often the victim of this wily fox? This fox, the hunter, himself finally hunted and killed?

Whatever the point of view of the person seeing the fox lying in the field, the judgment will be made according to the person's *value* system. And this *rational* method of *decision-making* describes the FEELING function. The ready, easy way one may *express* the feelings one has for the fox, the farmer, or the chickens is an attribute enjoyed mainly by those preferring the feeling over the thinking function.

Judging

There is *no ambiguity* in this image. Things are *organized, orderly, the way they ought to be.* "A place for everything, and everything in its place." You need *no more data* to understand the *meaning* behind this photograph. People working here go from *job* to *job, completing* one before tackling the next. A sense of *control,* of easy *final decision* prevails. The tasks involved are *specific, routine, clearly defined.* And so is the image. Both exemplify the JUDGING interface.

"Clearly defined" clearly defines the JUDGING function. *Efficient, functional, getting the job done,* these National elevators span the small towns of Saskatchewan. There is no doubt as to their *function.* One glance at the contrasting shadowy cylinders, patterned houses of grain, and the viewer knows what they are, and where he is. This *certainty,* this sense of *purpose, this patterning of formal beauty* typifies the JUDGING interface.

A precision system of clean, well-defined parts, the flawless spin of wheels, all orderly, all under control — all parts demanding *care* and *experience* to keep the machine in good *dependable* working order — is almost a JUDGING type's dream come true. Such a person might also very much enjoy this photo. Do you?

Perceiving

Just as the definiteness of the machine on page 91 appeals to a judging personality, the *ambiguity* of this landscape appeals to the PERCEIVING type. *Needing more data* before being able to make a decision, the perceiving attitude allows the view to put off a sense of closure, and *explore* the *infinite possibilities* of mood and meaning captured by the photographer's art. It may immediately occur to the judging type to ask, "Just what does this have to do with elevators?" The perceiving type may think of that question, but is quite likely to *abandon* it and fill his mind with *several* others.

An empty box car sits in an empty field. Is there a rail line linking it to the elevator? Why was it abandoned? Was it abandoned? And again the viewer is presented with the PERCEIVING attitude of *needing more information*. This *flexible, non-precise* nature of the image, its *lack of order* or *control* is what makes it so appealing to the perceiving inquisitive outlook on the external world.

Lack of planning, lack of closure, moving from project to project, these are the characteristics common to the PERCEIVING focus which too often drives judging types to distraction. "Three trees growing out of a clump of rocks in the middle of a clothesline? My God!" the judging type might exclaim in despair as the perceiving type only smiles. The trees are growing well, the clothes are on the line, a boat sits ready to provide a release from work, and grain elevators, full of rich grain, silhouetted against a moving sky. And life, with all its mystery, its *flexibility,* its *multi-faceted* nature, is wonderful!

The Intuitive is Future Oriented

3/In Other Words

I have turned to a variety of media experiences to present this overview of typology designed to stimulate the intuitive type. It is the nature of the intuitive to see relationships. Lovers of the symbolic and abstract, they sense implications and possibilities inherent within sensing experiences. The intuitive is often unwilling to accept things simply as they are. He must go beyond, behind, around, ahead of the experience.

This became very clear to me one morning when my teenage daughter, a sensing type, and I, an intuitive, were discussing a film, *Paul's Case*, which we had seen on TV the evening before. We had both enjoyed the film: I for the symbolism, the implied meanings; she for the wonderful detail of the photography, the action of the plot. We were discussing the suicidal death of the young man. "I wonder what would have happened if Paul had not killed himself, if he had returned to his hometown?" I mused. She looked at me with total disinterest.

"What difference does it make? He's dead."

"Yes, but what if. . . ." I ventured.

"Dead is dead," she replied, not unkindly. "I mean, the poor guy is dead."

Just so. The eye teaches the mind for the sensing type. Truly the mind teaches the eye for the intuitive.

The Archetype

The discovery of the archetype was possible because the intuitive mind processed data out of common patterns recurring in dreams, myths, legends, art, life. The notion of universal construct or idea, associated with symbols which would be similar for all cultures, at any time, is the usual interpretation of archetype. A primordial image is how Jung has described this construct. The same description can be applied to a definition of psychological type. This is, perhaps, due to the fact that the degree of psychological effectiveness of the primordial image is determined, according to Jung, by the individual's orientation to extraversion (Jung, 1971, p. 445). This orientation, in turn, directs the other psychological preferences. You may examine your own dreams to find archetypal patterns of psychological type preferences. A close friend shared with me an anxiety dream she often experienced. She is a highly acclaimed professor who travels about the world giving lectures and workshops. Her presentations are consistently brilliant and well prepared. Yet, before a conference, she often wakens in a cold sweat of panic. She dreams that she has arrived unprepared, with no instructional materials, and that she has had no time to prepare, and fails at her delivery. My friend is a judging type. Her need to organize carefully and prepare in advance is very strong. Even when her knowledge, her experience, her ten thousand well-prepared, well-organized, carefully filed copies of any materials she may need are readily available, she still dreams the nightmare common to her type — the nightmare of being confused, unprepared, disorganized, forced into a spontaneous, flexible, "wing it" mode. Yet this woman is indeed flexible, spontaneous, with more "wingingness" than she could ever need. But she needs more. She needs control over her environment, then the flexibility is free to, and does, exist. Her archetypal nightmare is a demonstration of the judging function in full focus.

In my own case, I dream that I will be on my way to a conference and I will become hopelessly lost. My anxiety mounts, and I become more confused, more lost. Finally, I abandon my car in desperation, beg rides from strangers — and realize I do not have an address for my destination. I think I remember the name of the hotel in which the conference is being held. But I may be wrong. I am. The strangers deliver me, minutes late, to the wrong hotel!

I am an intuitive perceiving type. Too often I have almost lived my nightmare. The archetypal shadow cast by my inferior function of sensation haunts my dreams.

I am not privy to your dreams. Once you have read *Insights* you may wish to write down your night travels and analyse them according to the archetypes of psychological type.

Television

Although we may not share common dreams, we probably share common house guests. Let us "intuitively" examine a few — "seeing" in them the various archetypes.

Archie Bunker, the lovable TV character, is an interesting embodiment of the conflict between a thinking type, Archie, and a feeling type,

Meathead. Part of Archie's charm as a character is that although he does use the thinking or analytical process, his data is so often wrong that his decisions or attitudes seem to defy reason. Archie analyses: the neighbor is black, blacks are dangerous, therefore I am in danger if I befriend my black neighbor. He does not allow his values, his personal response of actually liking his black neighbor to dissuade him. All, of course, to the consternation of his feeling-type son-in-law, who rationally uses his value system in decision-making. Feeling types often enjoy this example, especially when thinking types insist their process is more rational, or correct, or intellectual. Archie is rarely any of the above.

Rhoda's mother, Mrs. Morgenstern, is an example of the sensing judging (SJ) personality. She is so extreme in her "insistence" on having things "the way they ought to be" (her way) that she almost caricatures the type. However, those of us who have dealt with an SJ person in our families may smile at some of the similarities. "But, Maw," the girls wail as their mother lovingly, unflinchingly shapes, guides, redirects their love lives, their life-styles, their plans for the weekend. But pity the man, woman, or child attempting to harm either of her girls. An SJ's protective instinct and sense of responsibility are fiercely passionate and endlessly loyal.

Mork, space creature, comedian, extravert. He acts impulsively, without reflection. He "tries" everything. He learns by doing, risking all, accepting the chance involved with trial and error. Moreover he loves interaction, being vocal, and Mindy.

Quincy is also a judging type, fiercely protecting the innocent. Rockford is a typical intuitive perceiving type, working on hunches, getting himself into unplanned adventures. Can you type your favorite TV stars?

Works of Art

Artists have fed the intuitive mind with endless feasts of the symbolic, the abstract, the suggestive. I often rush to an art gallery pulling my too resistant daughter behind me. I seize upon the nearest, most concrete, most realistic painting I can spy and pose her in front of it, hoping it will please her sensing soul. I must confess that the one which has most pleased and fascinated her was a Salvador Dali. A tiny pinprick of a painting, it had to be viewed through a microscope. What seemed to be the head of Lincoln, upon closer inspection, turned out to be a painting of the Last Supper. Now there was the type of meaning within meaning that appealed to the sensing's love of detail.

Let me urge you to pause before these paintings as I attempt to uncover meaning within meaning.

Each one of us is often irritated by differences in others when those differences conflict with our plans, or preferred ways of doing things. "Why must he always be so fastidious?" We can be bothered, too, by the absence of certain traits in ourselves. "Why am I so often late for meetings?" And there are those times, too, when we very much admire those aspects of personality that others have and which we lack. "I, who am so unorganized, am really amazed at how quickly you schedule your affairs and manage to get everything done on time." It is from this vantage point I will explore the various aspects of psychological type as found in works of art, in pointing out those aspects of personality an opposite type can so admire, simply because it is not natural and easily available to him.

Extraversion:

The Attitudes

Introversion:

Rare is the introvert who has not looked wistfully at the extravert's easy relating and active physical interacting at a large gathering. This wonderful extraverted energy comes alive in John Leech's etching p. 104.

In contrast, extraverts admire in the introvert that reflective attitude which permits a natural thoughtfulness, a quiet determination. That powerful inner strength is obvious in Rodin's *The Thinker*, p. 105.

Sensing:

Ways of Perceiving

Intuition:

Immediate, simple, pure pleasure is the gift given those preferring the sensing function. Unlike the intuitive who too often sees the hidden promises, the inner allusions, the future complications of each event, the sensing type can open the senses, and enjoy the moment with a natural uncomplicated ease. Manet captures this revelry of the senses in *Luncheon on the Grass*, p. 106.

"Spiritual," "magical," "mysterious" describes the way the sensing type sees the intuitive. This powerfully creative, futuristic energy often perceived as being supernatural is imaginatively portrayed in Jean Delville's *Portrait of Mrs. Stuart Merrill*, p.107.

Thinking:

Feeling:
Ways of Making Decisions

In times of crisis, the feeling type might turn gratefully to the clear-sighted objective nature of the thinker. It is clear that *Clemenceau*, by Manet, p. 108, is aware of his own strong decisiveness.

Just as this decisive strength amazes the feeling type, so the feeler's easy ability to empathize fascinates the thinker.

The passion of Goya dramatically exemplifies the feeling type's powerful, natural energy turned towards the suffering of man. *"Si Son de otra linage,"* cries the artist — "Do they belong to another race?" p. 109.

Judging:

Perceiving:
Preferred Functions

"Decisive," "confident," "successful," describes those characteristics so attractive in the judging type. The sense of security, of certainty, so apparent in this portrait of an impeccably dressed Antonin Proust by Manet, p. 110, can be appreciated by any perceiving type.

In contrast, the judging type may envy the easy acceptance apparent in the face, the body of *Tipsy Woman*, by Manet, p. 111. "There may be much to be done," muses the perceiving type, "and maybe after this cigarette, this little dish of ice-cream, maybe then. . . ."

"Ah, to be so free," thinks the judging personality as he hurries on down the street.

Etching by John Leech, *Pictures of Life and Character*

"The Thinker" by Auguste Rodin

"Luncheon on the Grass" by Edouard Manet

"Portrait of Mrs. Stuart Merrill" by Jean Delville

"Portrait of Clemenceau" by Edouard Manet

"Si son de otro linage" by Francisco José de Goya

"Portrait of Antonin Proust" by Edouard Manet

"The Tipsy Woman" by Edouard Manet

Literature

What do you read, my lord?
Words, words, words
                    Hamlet

The bulk of this chapter offers several excerpts selected from a variety of biographies and novels. The literature was not especially selected because of any inclination on the part of the authors to reveal the archetype in their characters. The archetype naturally appears. The most commonly visible type is the intuitive. This may be because many writers are themselves intuitive types and they find this function easy to define in a myriad of ways.

The process of "seeing" the archetype of typology in a piece of literature is itself an intuitive process of reading between the lines. Initially the selections will be accompanied by explanations for the purpose of instruction and clarity. At the end of the chapter a few examples are presented for you to read and test your understanding of typology.

Autobiography

A logical place to start this "literature search" for the various types is with Jung himself. An extreme INTROVERT as a child, Jung expresses his discomfort with the extraverted world, and his preference for solitude.

> I return now to the discovery I made in the course of associating with my rustic classmates. I found that they *alienated me from myself.* (p. 19)
>
> . . . . .
>
> What had led me astray during the crisis was *my passion for being alone, my delight in solitude.* Nature seemed to me full of wonders, and I wanted to *steep myself* in them.*
>
>   Carl Jung, *Memories, Dreams, Reflections,* p. 32

In an interesting tale describing Freud's preoccupation with what he misconstrued as a deathwish directed towards Freud by Jung, Jung describes a dinner party at which Jung conveyed to Freud his fascination with the peat-bog corpses. Apparently Freud was horrified by this fascination and felt it meant that Jung secretly wished for Freud's death so that Jung might become Europe's leading psychoanalyst. In this excerpt from that story Jung reveals in himself the INTUITIVE trait of confusing details, but being intrigued by things unexplained.

---

*In all of these quotations the emphasis has been added to highlight the clue words to the preference discussed.

Having read about these peat-bog corpses, I recalled them when we were in Bremea, but, *being a bit muddled, confused them with the mummies in the lead cellars of the city.* This interest of mine got on Freud's nerves. "Why are you so concerned with these corpses?" he asked me several times.

Memories, p. 156

This interest of Jung's in things that were and might be, this endless thirst for knowledge — for in knowledge is truth and power — epitomizes an innovative scientific mind, the mind of an INTUITIVE THINKER.

Jung clarifies his own INTUITIVE THINKING focus:

I was concerned with *investigating truth*, not with questions of personal prestige.

Memories, p. 158

As well, Bertrand Russell's autobiography provides another illustration of an INTROVERTED, INTUITIVE THINKING type. His INTROVERSION, like Jung's, is made clear to the philosopher early in his life. He rarely trusted others with his innermost thoughts, and when he did, he wished he hadn't.

Throughout the greater part of my childhood, the most important hours of my day were those that *I spent alone in the garden*, and the most vivid part of my existence was *solitary.* I seldom mentioned my more serious thoughts to *others*, and when I did *I regretted it.*

Bertrand Russell, *Autobiography*, p. 25

His love of reason and his desire to base decisions upon the rational, THINKING process was so powerful in Russell, it persuaded him even when values and feeling taught from childhood were part of the consideration.

At this age (13 yrs) I began a *systematic investigation* of the supposed rational arguments in favour of fundamental Christian beliefs. I spent endless hours in *meditation* upon this subject; I could not speak to anybody about it for fear of giving pain. I suffered acutely both from the gradual loss of faith and from the need of silence. I thought that if I ceased to believe in God, freedom and immortality, I should be very, very unhappy. I found, however, that the *reasons* given in favour of these dogmas were very unconvincing.

Autobiography, p. 35

As the years progressed, Russell's faith in reason and mistrust of what he calls "instinct" or feeling (in Jungian terms) became more pronounced.

In all things I have made the vow to *follow reason*, not the instincts inherited partly from my ancestors and gained gradually by them, owing to a process of natural selection, and partly due to my education.

. . . this God-given conscience, which made Bloody Mary burn the Protestants, this is what we reasonable beings are to follow. I think this idea mad and I endeavour to go by *reason as far as possible*. What I take as my ideal is that which ultimately produces greatest happiness of greatest number. Then I can *apply reason* to find out the course most conducive to this end.

Autobiography, p. 47

This mistrust of "instinct" is not a mistrust of intuition. Russell was undoubtedly an INTUITIVE THINKING type. His love of scientific knowledge, the outstanding feature of the INTUITIVE THINKING personality, is revealed in this powerful statement:

There was a footpath leading across fields to New Southgate and I used to go there alone to watch the sunset and contemplate suicide. I did not, however, commit suicide, because I *wished to know more* of mathematics.

Autobiography, p. 38

Using Russell, the man, and quoting his writing as an example of the THINKING type of personality offers a clear opportunity to dispel the notion that thinking types lack passion or humanity. Russell was a giant humanitarian capable of extreme emotion. The opening line of his autobiography pays tribute to that fact.

Three passions, simple but overwhelmingly strong, have governed my life: *the longing for love*, the search for knowledge, and *unbearable pity* for the suffering of mankind.

Autobiography, p. 9

Russell continues to describe his search for, his passionate need of, his great joy in, love.

I have sought love, first, because it brings ecstasy–ecstasy so great that I would often have *sacrificed all the rest of life* for a few hours of this joy.

Autobiography, p. 9

Ah, you may exclaim, he is a FEELING type. To an extent, reader, you are right. Certainly Russell, such a full and experimental and sensitive man, developed all of his functions. His ability to express his emotions so well is ample evidence of this. But a careful examination of Russell's statement concerning love demonstrates that there is a THINKING explanation in-

volved. He seeks love ''BECAUSE'' it brings ecstasy. Reasonable?
Analytical? Full of emotion?

Yes. Yes. Yes.

History and literature are not comprised only of wonderful INTUITIVE
THINKING types. These types can conduct a ruthless pursuit of
knowledge — as does this professor of medicine captured in bizarre circumstances by Dylan in his play based on the life of the infamous scientist.

> I pledge you to adventure: I command you to experiment. Remember
> that the practice of Anatomy is absolutely vital to the *progress* of
> medicine. Remember that the *progress* of medicine is vital to the *pro-
> gress* of mankind. And mankind is *worth fighting for; killing and lying
> and dying for.* Forget what you like. Forget all I have ever told you.
> But remember that. . . .
>> Dylan Thomas, *The Doctor and the Devils*, p. 131

Thomas's character believed in and lived by his credo. For this man was
no other than the infamous Dr. Robert Knox, Edinburgh's nineteenth-
century anatomist and lecturer, who purchased bodies from men who
murdered for their goods. When discovered and exposed, as not the hero
of his century, but rather the villain, Dr. Knox mocked his own self-
destruction. In his mockery, much in contrast to Russell's appreciation, is
Knox's disregard for emotion.

> Would you have me death-dance and moan, like a Gaelic dip-
> somaniac at a distillery fire? Must tragedy go immediately to the feet
> and the tongue? Because *I can observe my history calmly* as it burns
> and topples around me, you *emotional gluttons* think yourselves
> cheated. ''Oh, he *can't feel* anything,'' you say. ''When we told him
> his life was over, he did not tear the relics of his hair or address the
> travelling moon in blank verse. He blew his nose and called for
> Burgundy.''
>> *The Doctor and the Devils*, p. 125

The extreme intuitive thinking type cannot be examined without a look
at its counterpart, the INTUITIVE FEELING type. The character I have
chosen to represent this type is also a giant of his era. His temperament
will be examined from the point of view of his whole personality. In this
way you may get a glimpse of how each aspect of psychological type
relates, in a unique fashion, with every other aspect. The character you
are about to meet is an EXTRAVERTED, INTUITIVE, FEELING, PERCEIV-
ING (ENFP) type.

The ENFP temperament is prone to be ''enthusiastic,'' ''innovative,''
''creative.'' When that temperament exists in a creative genius, living on
the borders of sanity, it tends to provide both an extreme and a

fascinating look at the ENFP. Because of his eccentric mental and physical nature, it is risky to make any absolute statements about Nijinsky's psychological preference. The ideas expressed here merely speculate on the particular perspective which Nijinsky, and perhaps creative artists like him, might have towards their art and their lives.

EXTRAVERSION is made clear early in the diary when, as Nijinsky compares himself with God, he expresses his extraverted love of action:

> I look like Him, only He has a calm gaze, and my eyes look round. I am a man, *OF MOTION*, not one of immobility. I have different habits from Christ. He loved immobility, and I love *motion and dancing*.
> R. Nijinsky, ed., *The Diary of Vaslav Nijinsky*, p. 5

Although he writes his diary, Nijinsky prefers the spoken word:

> I will tell the whole truth, and others will continue what I have begun. I am like Zola, but *I want to speak* and not write novels.
> *Diary*, p. 28

And true to all extraverts, to all people, there are moments when Nijinsky prefers to be alone:

I like to hide from people; I am used to living alone. But the true pain behind those words becomes clear as he adds:

> Maupassant was terrified of being lonely. The Count of Monte Cristo liked loneliness because he wanted time to prepare for his revenge. Maupassant was frightened of solitude; he loved people. *I am afraid of loneliness* but will not cry.
> *Diary*, p. 177

Even stronger than his plea for action, for extraversion, is his love of, his fascination for, his ultimate trust in, INTUITION. This passion is expressed over and over again throughout the diary:

> I am feeling through the flesh and not through the intellect. I am the flesh. I am the *feeling*. I am God in flesh and feeling. I am man and not God. I am simple. *I need not think.* I must make myself felt and *understood through feeling*. Scientists think about me and break their heads, but their thinking will not give any results. They are stupid.
> *Diary*, p. 6

Although in the quotation above, Nijinsky uses the terminology "feeling" as opposed to "thinking", it is intuition (in the Jungian sense) and not feeling (in the Jungian sense) that is meant. When one refers to a method of perceiving, it is always either sensation or intuition which is being discussed. Feeling and thinking (again, I am speaking strictly as Jung coined the terms) always refer to the decision-making process.

He uses the terms often, in complaining, for example, about his wife's lack of intuition:

> She *thinks too much*, and therefore *has no feeling*. I am not afraid of her leaving me but I will not marry again. (p. 9-10)

And finally, Nijinsky speaks exactly the language of the intuitive, of the man for whom the mind tells the eye:

> I speak of things I have never seen, but *I can see without using my eyes*. I am feeling. Blind people will understand me if I tell them that *eyes are not longer needed.*
>
> *Diary*, p. 153

Nijinsky comes closer to a description of feeling in the Jungian sense when he describes his relationship with Diaghilev. Also, he gives a very FEELING reason for his choice not to work in the cinema; his decision is not based on logical analysis, but on a value system.

> I know cinematography. I wanted to work in the films, but I understood their meaning. *The cinema is used in order to breed money*, and this is used to breed the cinema industry. *I understood that the cinema brings profit only to few men, and the theater to many.* The work in the theater is very hard for me, but I prefer privation to the work in the films. Diaghilev told me many a time that one should invent something on the lines of the cinema for dancing, because its force is great. Bakst, a well known Russian painter, a Jew, said that films were good from a money point of view. I did not say anything, because I felt that Bakst and Diaghilev thought that I was but a boy and therefore kept my thoughts. Diaghilev always looks for logic in thoughts. I know that thought without logic has no value, *but logic cannot exist without feeling.*
>
> *Diary*, p. 52

Nijinsky, true to his type, reveals many examples of empathy and compassion:

> He told me that his father was once angry with him and he cannot even now forget his anger until today. The doctor's distorted face made me feel the offense of his father. *I almost cried.* I was sorry. *I do not know whom to pity more, the son or the father.*
>
> *Diary*, p. 43

As a PERCEIVING type, Nijinsky explicitly defines his preference for finding information, which is a perceiving attribute, over his desire to control, a judging characteristic.

> I do not write to argue or reason, but to *explain*. I want to help
> mankind, and am not boasting about my book, because I do not
> know what to write.
>
>   *Diary*, p. 113

It is in his "nature" to want to explain, and to use intuition to do it.
And he did it best through the dance. This is where his genius will never
be forgotten.

As Nijinsky revealed his creative genius through the dance, Sylvia
Ashton-Warner has given the world the artistry of her teaching and her
writing. With wonderful honesty and intense insight Ashton-Warner has
written of the ways and whys of both her organic teaching and her private
world. Excerpts from her writing exemplify the most creative type of all,
the INTROVERTED, INTUITIVE, FEELING, PERCEIVING type.
Introversion:

> But what I love best is to *wander alone* around strange corners, into
> downstairs import shops among exotic people, selling their foreign
> wares; to wait at thundering intersections, *anonymous in the crowds*.
> In the thick of it.
>   Sylvia Ashton-Warner, *I Have Passed This Way*, p. 475

Introverts crave this time alone, faceless, as a means of centring their
own energies inward, where it feels best.
Introversion:

> I wasn't aware of my *untouchability*, both inward and physical.
>   *I Have Passed*, p. 77

It is difficult for introverts to trust their world, to feel accepted by it.
Intuition:

> I *don't see* any danger, only *feel* it, sharply gruesome in each beat of
> my pulse.
>   *I Have Passed*, p. 73

Intuitives sense impressions, only unconsciously aware of the source of
those impressions.
Intuition:

> I paused. I'd *lost the thread*. With elbow on table I covered my eyes
> with a hand while I tried to find it again but all I *could see in my
> mind* were canoes, drowned men, eels and a grandfather. "What was
> I talking about, Tiny?"
>   *Myself*, p. 22

It is a common thing for the mind of the intuitive to wander, to move to new ideas in a stream-of-consciousness manner.
Intuitive Feeling:

> Emotionally I was *lawless* with an outsized *compulsion to dream* and a personal morality that barely coincided at any point with the prevailing Victorianism.
>
> *I Have Passed*, p. 77

Here Ms. Ashton-Warner reveals that quality of the NF personality which almost forces her to be authentic to her own particular values and inspirations.
Intuitive Perceiving:

> I did not know that Norma and I shared *secret scenarios* ad infinitum when we had to get the cow. We were not trudging along a country road but riding restive Arab steeds "of impatient hoof" and "snuffing the breezy wind," and we were dressed in velvet. Or we were travelling in a mini-train on rails set in the grass on the roadside. It made going to get the cow worthwhile. Our *fantasy did not supply the detail* of how we managed to drive the cow home if we were riding a train. In reality we were quite capable of driving the cow right past the home gate *forgetting to bring her in*. It was only the cow herself wanting to be milked who noticed the gate and paused there in wistful hope and doubt.
>
> *I Have Passed*, p. 28

And here we see the quality of losing sight of reality in the pure delight of fantasy. This is typical of the NP combination.
Perceiving:

> We younger children loved the part where *she kept on getting up and going somewhere else, willy-nilly regardless. We loved "shifting."* New places to find, new things to do, new rivers to swim in, new horses to ride.
>
> *I Have Passed*, p. 17

The perceiving interface often shows up as a love for adventure, for change, for a chance to experience the new and the different.
Perceiving:

> The important step forward in my work was that I'd tried myself out to confirm what I'd thought, that numbers meant nothing and that I was quite at home on the stage; it meant that I was ready to take on any university job training young people with *no preparation or equipment*

at all. As long as somebody else did the organisation. Just put the
people in front of me and I'd do the rest.

I Have Passed, p. 445

And here we have the perceiving function at its best, spontaneous,
open, loving the process, leaving the onerous task of preparation to the
judging types who don't find it in the least burdensome.

As the NFP must be free to create, the SENSING, FEELING, PERCEIVING
types (SFP) must be free to do whatever thing they do best. ISFP types are
often wonderful performing artists. Elvis Presley is an example of such a
type. So is, ladies and gentleman, the incredible Bette Midler.

Because I have filled this section with examples of intuition (the world
of literature being so full of them), allow me to pluck gratefully from the
gutsy words of the lady herself, a few examples of the SENSING function
in action:

Dizzy with exhilaration and dread, I took my favorite Paper Mate in
hand and began to do what I *always do* in a situation that demands
bold and forthright action: *I made lists.*

Bette Midler, *A View From A Broad,* p. 19

Sensing types are great list makers, but it takes an outrageous Bette
Midler to include such items as: "1. Learn to decline in Seven tongues.
2. Buy a glove. Study it. 3. Keep this information secret."

Bette's earliest memories of her childhood are full of sensation and practical reality.

My first *memories* of Hawaii are *of oleander bushes* that surrounded
our apartment house. Their flowers gave off a *sweet* — almost too
sweet — *smell,* and the *white milk* that spilled all over your clothes if
you picked them was *impossible to remove.*

A View From A Broad, p. 40

Bette emphasizes the SENSING attitude in a letter to her sister,
probably an intuitive type. She scolds her for not paying attention,
makes lists for her to follow, gives directions so explicit that only a
sensing type could ever remember them, is amazingly practical (even
in all her madness), is painfully shy (in true introverted fashion)
about asking her sister to join her. But is even more painfully
precise. Only a sensing type would specify "prayer" time in her
sister's home on the morning of September 18. Because of copyright, I
must suggest instead that you read this letter for youself in *A View From a
Broad,* page 50.

But what I can use to demonstrate sensation in action is a letter written much in the same fashion by my ISFP daughter during her first week away from home. September 1st found Mickey attending a Quaker boarding in the Kootney mountains of northern British Columbia. This is the letter I received:

Dear Mom:

A whole week has gone by since you drove me up here to the top of the middle of nowhere. Surprise, surprise — I'm enjoying it, so far, except for algebra. My room-mates, Sue and John, were both here last year and are a big help in introducing me to the other kids and making sure I get involved. Their only cruelty is in insisting I clean up my share of the room *every* day.

Now this next part is important so I want you to concentrate. Maybe you should pin this to the fridge.

1. The goldfish, Sammy — his life depends on you. Is he still alive? Remember to feed him one coffee measure of the green Hartz food every other day — in the morning. And once a week, a teaspoon of the shrimp meal, in the red package with yellow letters. Both are in the left hand cupboard over the sink. And change his water every Saturday. He likes Willie Nelson music, so play one of his records every couple of days.

2. I left my black travel alarm in the dresser, in my socks drawer, bottom right. Would you bring it next time you come — which will be soon, I hope (and not just because I need the clock — I don't really, because Sue has one, but I'd like my own).

3. Give Corky the wonder dog lots of kisses from me and what's more, play lots of ball with him. Get Verne to fix the gate so he can't run out front and get flattened by a truck.

Don't worry about me, I'll survive. The kids here are a lot nicer than at any other school, and so are the teachers. Get lots of beauty rest so you'll be fresh for the next big drive to Argenta.

I must chuckle as I include it, anticipating the astonishment my daughter will experience upon reading this.

Not only is she exactly the same *size* as Better Midler, not only was she born on the same *day* as her favorite singer/heroine, and not only does her personality type seem to be identical, but she also shows similar traits to her heroine in her letter writing. I trust this indulgence will serve the purpose not only of pleasing her, but of informing the reader.

If, by the way, you are wondering why I would suggest that a lady as wildly outrageous as Bette Midler is an introvert, the answer lies in her own words.

The ladies I dream up are *masks I can hide behind. And I like hiding.*
And I like masks. In fact, I love masks.

A View From A Broad, pp. 44-45

Many a "performing" character, be it a classroom clown, a professional
actress, the "life-of-the-party," is truly an introvert in disguise.

Fiction

Just as the examples of psychological type appear in autobiographical
works, so too, are they apparent in works of fiction. Perhaps it is a
disguised blessing that the intuitive function emerges more often than any
other of the preferences, for intuition is the most difficult aspect of the
typology to describe. It must be experienced, recognized. Hopefully, by
the end of this chapter you will understand the evasive, irrational process
of which this chapter is directed. Hopefully, you too can cry "Eureka!"

> Call it intuition, divine influence, or plain dumb luck — any way you
> sliced it, it was still eureka. Eureka! Surely, Leigh-Cheri hadn't ex-
> pected to solve cosmic riddles by consulting a book on package
> design. She merely *had a . . . hunch . . .* that such a book might
> enlighten her about the reasons for there being pyramids on the
> Camel pack. As it turned out, there was *scant information*, but it was
> *pertinent enough to make her cry "Eureka!"*
>
> Tom Robbins, *Still Life With Woodpecker*, p. 181

An INTUITIVE PERCEIVING wife relies on her sensing judging husband:

> I climbed more steps to a small pavilion where people were looking at
> a view. You weren't there. A park with many paths spread out behind
> me. "Michael!" I called . . . You had the maps, all the Italian money,
> the keys to the pensione, whose name I could not even remember!
> How casually (because I knew you liked being in charge) had I hand-
> ed over all responsibility to you. I could not even remember the name
> of the street the pensione was on. Now I really had something to cry
> about. "Michail!"
>
> Audrey Thomas, *Latakia*, p. 93

An INTUITIVE FEELING type projects onto her husband her own idealized attitude to love and the trap it often snares its victims into:

> I have made up a new verb, Michael — "pedestal-ize" . . . Anyway,
> you pedestalized me, my dear, *as all Romantics do* to their women,
> and so there was no place to go but down. *I kept telling you I had
> feet of clay, but you wouldn't listen.* You believed in "the marriage of
> true minds" and forgot that that guy also wrote "My mistress' eyes are
> nothing like the sun."
>
> *Latakia*, p. 45

And I'm a Romantic too, Michael. I *idealized you* as well. Then, in February, cynical Robert wrote: "So in the cold light of dawn, the Prince turned out to be only a frog after all."

Latakia, p. 47

If you are an NF, you may recognize the agony of "pedestalizing" your loved one. Here is a FEELING type, having a difficult time dealing with the negative aspects of responsibility:

They scrambled up very eagerly and followed her close. Mrs. Thompson tried to imagine what they had been up to; she did not like the notion of Mr. Helton taking it on himself to correct her little boys, but *she was afraid to ask them for reasons.* They might tell her a lie, and *she would have to overtake them in it, and whip them.* Or she would have to pretend to believe them, and they would get in the habit of lying. Or they might tell her the truth, and it would be something she would have to whip them for. *The very thought of it gave her a headache.*

Katherine Anne Porter, "Noon Wine,"
in *The Collected Stories of Katherine Anne Porter,* p. 238

An INTUITIVE trying to remember something:

I couldn't remember. Something about cowboys? Yes? No? *I couldn't remember. . . . Something about cowboys. It was on the tip of my tongue.*

Latakia, p. 94

An INTROVERTED SENSING THINKING type answering a question:

He laughed, and *began to consider what she meant before he replied.*

"I don't know-whether-it made me feel anything," he replied *deliberately, pondering over his answer, as usual. . . .*

"Why!" he admitted, laughing, and trying to tell the *exact truth,* "I thought how *pretty* your hands are — and what they are like to touch — and I thought it was a new experience to *feel* somebody's hair tickling my cheek."

From "The White Peacock" in *D. H. Lawrence,* p. 463

It seems many INTUITIVE PERCEIVING women become annoyed with the caution of their THINKING JUDGING mates:

You talked a lot about "taking risks." You're a very good poker player; you won a lot of money off those fellows on the ship. I think you take *calculated risks;* I think you make sure you cover your bets.

Latakia, p. 132

For a final example in this series, I would like to present the trait that haunts and motivates the INTUITIVE FEELING type, the need to be genuine, to be true to oneself, at all costs. It has guided me in each step of writing this book, as I have attempted not to distort truth for the sake of clarity. Whew! It hasn't been easy. But it is a powerful force — and it is felt by INTUITIVE FEELING types regardless of their "place in life," their "moral attitude to society." It is expressed during an interview between Nicole and Norman Mailer. Nicole is the "wife" of Gary Gilmore, and the woman over whom he claims to have shot two men.

> She seemed to have a *commitment* to the interviews as deep as the beating of her heart. It was as if she had to tell him the story as once she had told it to Gary, and tell it all, tell it not to satisfy her guilt (and sometimes he thought she felt very guilty), no, tell for some deeper reason. . . . "*Nothing is worse in all the world than the taste of bullshit in your mouth.*"
>
> Norman Mailer, *The Executioner's Song*, p. 1010

Identifying Types: A Quiz

And now, it's your turn. Read the following passages. There is an example of each of the eight categories of psychological type represented. Use your *sensing* function to seek out details that will give a clue; and then go with your hunch, or *intuitive* function, in seeing the overall pattern. Try as you do this little exercise to be aware of the manner in which you *process* information.

A. Which of these exemplifies Extraversion, which Introversion?

1. Why can't I give myself the pleasure of having people around me? It's a necessity for me to see young, lively, happy people, free people burning with a desire to do something.
   Arthur Miller, Adaptation of Ibsen's *An Enemy of The People*, p. 25

2. Do you passionately examine yourself, ruthlessly analyze yourself, do you agonize as I did between feeling and reason? Do you know the need to sit in silence over a thing, to follow a line of thought to a firm conclusion, then write down that conclusion? Do you retreat into solitude and consult your instinct when logic leaves you high and dry?
   Sylvia Ashton-Warner, *Myself*, p. 1

This is an example of

_____

This is an example of

_____

B. Which of these exemplifies Sensing, which Intuition?

3. I'm amazed at the notes, mental and actual, that were being taken. I put my hand over yours and said, "I love you, Michael." I was looking at you and smiling. At the same time, I heard the young dejected sailor order "una cerveaz" and noticed that the beer he was given was called "Tropical."

Audrey Thomas, *Latakia*, p. 73

4. Her hope of being a beauty died hard, until the notion of being a jockey came suddenly and filled all her thoughts. Quietly, blissfully, at night before she slept, and too often in the daytime when she should have been studying, she planned her career as a jockey. It was dim in detail, but brilliant at the right distance.

Katherine Anne Porter, "Old Mortality" in *The Collected Stories of Katherine Anne Porter*, p. 196

This is an example of

_____

This is an example of

_____

C. Which of these shows a Thinking and which a Feeling way of making decisions?

5. If then that friend demand why Brutus rose against Caesar, this is my answer: Not that I lov'd Caesar less, but that I lov'd Rome more. Had you rather Caesar were living and die all slaves, than that Caesar were dead, to live all free men? As Caesar lov'd me, I weep for him; as he was fortunate, I rejoice at it; as he was valiant, I honour him; but, as he was ambitious, I slew him. There is tears for his love; joy for his fortune; honour for his valour; and death for his ambition.

William Shakespeare, *Julius Caesar*, Act 3, scene 2, lines 20-30

6. Yes, ma'am. I had opportunities to! — But I — always thought of my mother . . . I always asked myself, would she or would she not — think — this or that person was — decent!

Tennessee Williams, *The Rose Tatoo*, p. 62

This is an example of

_____

This is an example of

_____

D. Which is a Judging and which a Perceiving interface?

7. The clock was old and confused, striking at random, confusing the hours. Hero hated it because the face said one thing and the voice another. For her it upset the march of the day. 'Crock-crok,' said the clock at half-past three.

"Don't you mind what the clock says?" she asked Eleanor. "I don't notice it." "I notice it," said Hero. She liked everything to be quite clear and defined.

Rumer Godden, *Gone: A Thread of Stories*, p. 186

Hero exemplifies

8. I understand that obsession, that desire to get something finished and out of the way, but I think we took it to ridiculous extremes. Always to spend only an hour for lunch. Never to stay too long in the square on Saturday night. (In fact, we only stayed out at Aorba's once.) It wasn't any fun, Michael — there was no spontaneity.

Audrey Thomas, *Latakia*, p. 69

The speaker, unlike Michael, exemplifies

Were you right?

1. Here we have an EXTRAVERTED attitude in abundance. "Pleasure" of "people around me," "burning desire to DO something," both are so strong in this character we can almost feel the need and the energy. It is very-outward moving.

2. Here we find an example of the INTROVERTED attitude in process. The self-examination, the introspection, the "need to sit in silence," the retreating into "solitude," all show the introvert's need to be alone in order to reflect, particularly when a conflict is involved. It is interesting to note that the confict from which Sylvia Ashton-Warner is suffering is her mistrust of logic, and indeed, as we have seen, she is an example of the purest intuitive feeling process. Functions do not exist in isolation. Again, if you had labelled this as an example of intuition (reversing examples 6 and 1) you would be correct. "Instinct" would be your key word to clue you that this is also an example of intuition. I chose introversion because I focussed on a different set of words. Either choice is equally acceptable.

3. This woman marvels at her SENSING function. As a writer she must notice details, use her senses all the time. She is shocked at herself when she realizes she does it even as she is whispering words of love to her husband.

4. This is an example of a daydreaming INTUITIVE type. Other types daydream, but intuitives seem particularly prone to this type of reverie. The biggest clue is found in the final line. A sensing type's daydream would have plenty of detail, and in all likelihood would be oriented in the present tense. The key words here, then, are "dim in detail" and "at the right distance." If you had homed in on the words "quietly, blissfully, at night before she slept," you may have labelled this as an example of introversion. And you would be correct — the woman is probably an introverted intuitive type. Each of us is a combination of four different categories.

5. Brutus has made a rational THINKING decision, charged with emotion. His plea is full of passion. His act was passionate. But the underlying motive was objective reason. His ultimate desire was for justice, even at the price of terrible disharmony. The decision to murder Caesar was based on a LOGICAL ANALYSIS of the facts — "as he was ambitious, I slew him." Although Brutus is predominantly using the THINKING function, he clearly also utilizes his value system, his feeling function, as part of the decision — "(It is) not that I loved Caesar less, but that I loved Rome more." This is the noble act of a *mature* man who could sacrifice even his own safety for the common good of the citizens of Rome.

6. This is an example of the FEELING function in operation, not because it deals with the powerful emotions of young love, but because the young man has made a decision based on his value system. He considers his mother, her opinion, her feelings as part of the data he must consider before accepting the responsibility of love-making. This is a very thoughtful rational process, differing from the thinking process only in that, instead of analysis of the facts, subjective values provide the criteria for decision-making.

7. A JUDGING type, Hero "liked everything to be quite clear and defined." This is the giveaway. What Eleanor, the intuitive perceiving type, tends not even to notice, drives Hero to distraction. We can guess that Hero's close attention to detail speaks of a sensing preference. Her annoyance with the non-synchronization of the clock reveals her judging function. Things are not the way they ought to be.

8. This is a PERCEIVING wife becoming exasperated with judging-type husband who insists on scheduling their lives. Her discomfort with the time limits, "*always* to spend *only* an hour at lunch," "*never* to stay too long," show her preference for the perceiving function. The big giveaway, of course, is her plea for "spontaneity."

The Intuitive Type

The Judging Type

The Feeling Type

The Sensing Type

Pure Pleasure

People, whatever their differences, share a sensitivity to, and pleasure in, the striking visual image. This section contains three sets of photographs to delight the intuitive, particularly the intuitive-feeling types. No explanation is offered with each photo. They speak for themselves.

Carousel

Softly

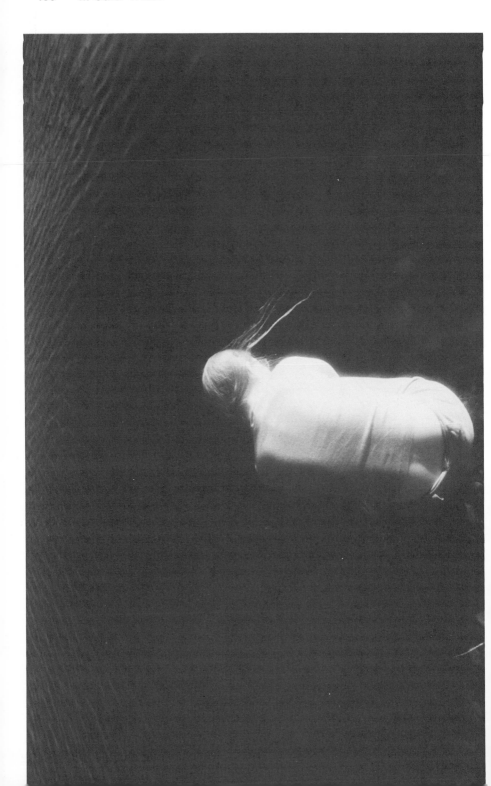

Shared Moments

A few years ago James struck upon an interesting idea. He realized a sense of communication in the process of photographing. Not merely the communication of an idea which the viewer of the image enjoys later, after development; but, in addition, a far more powerful, more immediate communication — the *communication between* the person being photographed and the photographer, at the very moment the shutter is clicked.

James felt this so strongly that it occurred to him that it might be evident in the images themselves. He began a new pattern in his career. He would photograph a person – a man at a fair, a woman on a bus, a friend sharing a cup of coffee. And immediately he would hand his camera over to the person he had just photographed and ask that person to photograph him.

The moments we have chosen to share with you are of James and his wife, because there are several of these, and you can see a variety of moods in the common theme of this couple. In James' own words, "In a fashion that is uniquely possible with photography, I have allowed the subject, the picturemaker, and the picture-making to become one, inseparable within that moment of time."

Observe how clearly mood and feeling dominate. Look at the eyes. Is there not a communion, an empathy, a sharing? No one said, "OK, let's now have a happy picture. A serious one. Pensive now, everyone." But it HAPPENED, a mood in time and space captured and shared almost magically.

Somehow, perhaps intuitively, perhaps in an irrational non-linear fashion, some information was transmitted and received. And a decision was made. That decision was clearly based on a sudden understood value being communicated and shared. A direct benefit of the feeling preference is a sense of empathy, a need for harmony. The process, then, is one of a personal value system being the unconscious basis of decision-making. The outcome is empathy, harmony, easy expression of feeling. The product becomes these moments in time.

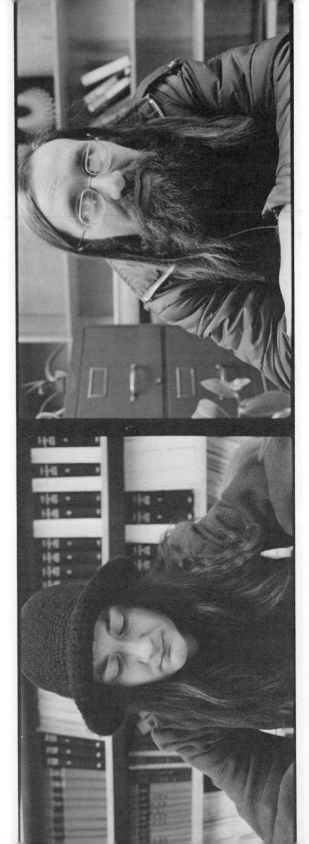

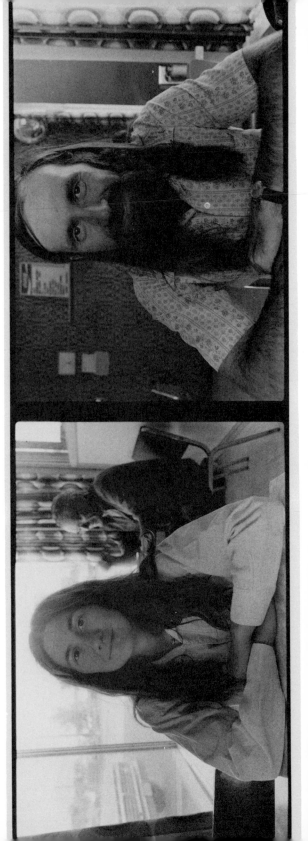

**The Feeling Type Is Very Good at Empathy/Aware of
People's Feelings/Can Easily Express His Emotions**

4/A Rose Is a Rose Is a Rose

Ice Fishing

Four years old, the girl was. And her mother's boy friend offered to prove his deep paternal nature. He packed Selma and Moose, his big New-foundland, into his black Buick and headed for Emma Lake. Ice-fishing. The mother waved a weak good-bye. Selma could barely see her; Moose, though full grown, still considered himself a puppy. The 150-lb. puppy now occupied more than his share of the front seat. Refusing to sit alone in the back, he had playfully leaped over the girl's shoulder, his huge body sprawling everywhere. She peeked at the disappearing figure of her mother through a forest of curly hair. She sneezed. Moose sniffed her face affec-tionately. His nose was cold, wet. It felt wonderful. He felt wonderful. He smelled wonderful. So did Selma. They smelt and felt one another happily. Two excited puppies.

Dan set up their camp. He chopped a huge hole in the ice. Crack. Selma ran, in a panic, toward the car. Moose sailed behind her. They ran, slipping, sliding, in a mad race with the ice. They were almost at the car before Dan caught up with them. He was laughing like an asshole.

"Hey, the ice always cracks like that. It ain't opening. It's OK. Hold on, you two."

Neither child nor dog was sure. They hadn't been sure from the minute they'd left the shore. Selma had tested each step, edging her way cautious-ly behind Dan. She had prayed, secretly to the River, apologizing for disturbing its rest, begging it not to kill them.

Even Moose, always so sure-footed, hadn't known how to walk. He kept sliding on clear patches or getting stuck in the deep snow banks, fighting to get free, almost like a swimmer struggling to stay on the surface of rough waters.

Dan eased the nervousness of his charges. He lit a fire, bribed them with fat red sausages. Everyone shared carefully, licking their chops. They laugh-ed at the terrible face Dan made when he took a drink from his whiskey bottle. They all drank from a large thermos of hot tea. Moose loved tea.

Dan poured some whiskey into a small bowl. Moose snuck up on the saucer of rye as if he were a cat, as if the whiskey were a still mouse. "Woo." He stuck his tongue in and out. His tongue was long and pink. "Woo." He slapped at the mouse saucer. It went spiraling across the ice. "Woo," said Moose again.

Selma was glad. She didn't want Moose acting the way Dan was. Dan kept dropping the red and white spoon he was attaching to the end of his line. His movements seemed jerky and sleepy. It was getting dark.

"Got anythin' yet?" Dan called over his shoulder as he rummaged for a fresh minnow.

The child peered into the hole. She had the large black mackinaw over her head and shoulders to darken the hole as Dan had shown her. That way she could see to the bottom. The lake was clear. The spoon moved when she jerked it.

Flash. A green shadow darted by the line. The child caught her breath. She jerked the line frantically. Another flash. She leaned over as far as she could, straining to catch another glimpse of the sacred promise. Fish.

Blue. Incredible blue. With sun shining through the ice. That's all she saw. That's all she thought. At least that's all she could remember thinking.

Years later, she confided to me that it wasn't what you'd think. Cold. Panic. Bursting lungs. A frantic searching for the ice-hold, fingernails clawing the rugged surface of frozen unyielding lake. It was all those later. In memory. In the cold wet sweat of nightmare. It still is.

But then it was the incredible blue. Everywhere. She was part of it. It was indivisible from her being. She yielded to its completeness. Its perfection.

When, suddenly, he had her. In his huge mouth. Moose was pulling the child, limp, from the icy waters. His breath was warm. He smelled wonderful.

* * *

FISH

Four years old the boy was. Big nuff. Big nuff to come along this time. Rolf always got to come. Rolf even got to feed the dogs, to throw them the raw fish, all frozen and slimy and fresh from the Indian's net. Rolf had always been Nancy's favorite. He went everywhere with her. He was only two years older than Sammy but he got to go everywhere. "Wait 'till you're older, Sam, then you can come too."

Well, this year he was older. And this year he had come to watch Nancy win the race. His sister. The only girl in the race. And she had the best dogs too. Rolf knew how much Nancy wanted to win. She had almost won last year. Almost. Everyone had laughed at the skinny fourteen-year-old running and wailing behind that pack of Malamutes. They had stopped laughing though, when she had come in second.

All summer she had trained. She had even traded her horse for a new dog. Wolf. And he was, mostly, just that — wolf. The old man who sold the dog to her warned her, "Don't feed them dogs too much. They eat before that race, they lazy, don't run. Keep 'em hungry, they run real good."

And Nancy had. The dogs were healthy. But for the last three days, no food had been thrown their way. They whined and tugged at the traces. They were nervous. Energy was everywhere. And they were ravenous. Somehow they knew that at the end of the race was food. They wanted to get on with it.

The old Indian was right. Six hours later the proudest fifteen-year-old in all Saskatchewan collapsed into the back of her Dad's old VW van. "Feed them dogs, Rolf, they deserve it. They're winners!"

"Yippee!"

"Oh, be careful, they're touchy — their feet's cut up pretty bad." The warning trailed into the boy's shouts of joy.

Rolf reached into the frozen sack. He hauled out two handsful of fish. Wolf was first in line. His teeth snarled back in impatience. "Just wait a minute," laughed the boy, enjoying the new victory, savoring the privilege of being the "giver of awards." Sammy looked on at his old brother in admiration and envy.

"Can I help, can I give 'em just one?"

In a sudden flow of generosity Rolf threw the fish. Away from Wolf. Towards his younger brother. Sammy saw the fish fly through the air. Saw the sudden anger and surprise leap into the dog's eyes. Saw the dog leap through the air. Saw the dog smash into his suddenly small, pale six-year-old brother. Saw the fish fly. Saw a scream uncoil itself in the air, hang there, suspended.

Wolf had dragged Rolf to the pack before anyone had even see that scream land. Rolf may have been dead before the other dogs attacked him. The first lunge had landed on the boy's neck. Blood was everywhere.

And now the boy was twenty; the girl twenty-two. No longer children, they were attending university in New York. And it was midnight. They knew it was late for them to be out walking. They knew they shouldn't be near Washington Square Park at this time of night. But Sammy and Selma were tired. They had studied late. So they took the short cut. They were complaining bitterly about professors who put books on reserve at the library. "They never have to stay at that damn building all night to get the books read."

"They can afford their own books," Selma added.

"And cars," lamented Sammy. "This walking is. . . ."

Sammy's voice was disappearing. His head was cocked to one side, ears straining. Selma turned just in time to see the shadow. Sammy had seen it too.

"Oh, God," she sighed in relief, "it's a dog."

Her voice was swallowed by a scream. It sounded like a child's scream. It was coming from Sammy's gaping mouth. It hung suspended in the air.

* * *

A rose is a rose is a rose. But a shadow of a dog is not a shadow of a dog. Same dog. Same shadow. But Sammy and Selma did not see that shadow with the same eyes, the same nerve endings, the same memories.

Perceptions. They color our world. They paint it many different colors. Knowing their stories helps you to understand how Sammy and Selma see the world.

How we all see the world is a product of every experience we have ever had. It is a product of our molecular structures. It is a product of our heritage. And it is, too, a product of our psychological preferences. Typologies can explain only a part of how we come to understand things. Whether they use their senses or their intuition, Sammy and Selma will see different worlds because they have lived separate lives. One cannot expect to understand everything about another person just by knowing his psychological preferences. But one can expect to understand one more facet of the wonderfully complex and fascinating aspect of human nature known as personality.

The greatest value of a knowledge of psychological type for the feeling type is that it helps people understand one another better. It provides that clue to understanding too often missing when our communication systems break down. The "magic" clue being provided is insight into the other's point of view.

As a means of examining this communication process a series of hypothetical situations are presented in this chapter. Each is analysed in Jungian terms and an interpretation of the communication breakdown is offered. It is not essential that you, the reader, feel comfortable with all the suggested interpretations. Indeed, it is unlikely that you will, particularly if it is a point of view determined by a function which is your least preferred way of viewing the world. Relax and accept this as a natural reaction for the present. Hopefully, it will be useful to examine the interactions from two points of view: first, it is hoped the reader will see the psychological functioning from another vantage point and will therefore better understand it; second (and ideally, perhaps), a peek into the world of other folks may allow readers insight into their own patterns of interaction.

"The World of Communication"

An Introvert Talks with an Extravert

An extraverted wife, Martha, returns home from a day's nursing. She is tired. Her introverted husband, Bill, is tired, too. It has been a long week and he is looking forward to being away from the office for a few days.

Martha: Tired, whew, I'm beat.
(She flops into a chair and puts her feet onto the ottoman. She groans.)
Bill: Me, too.
(He sits on the floor beside his wife and rubs her aching feet affectionately.)
    Guess we won't have to go to the banquet tonight — thank God.
(Martha takes her foot away. She sits up straight.)
Martha: The party, I forgot.
(She jumps up, rushing towards the bathroom.)
    I have to set my hair.
Bill: But you said you were beat.
(He looks baffled.)
Martha: (Already washing her hair)
    Watcha say?
Bill: I'm tired.
(He isn't sure why, but he's a bit angry.)
Martha: You'll feel better once we get there.
(Bill throws Martha a disparaging glance and switches on the TV. He is silent.)

The banquet does not go well. They come in one half hour late (Martha's hair not being dry on time) and have to trip through the entire banquet hall to find seats. Martha loves it. She "hi's" and hugs everyone in sight. These are her friends and although she sees them at work every day she seems delighted to see them again. Bill does not. He mumbles a few hellos and tries to get out of the limelight as fast as possible. He wishes his wife would stop her endless greetings and he hopes he can find a seat near Thomas who loves to fish, as Bill does. Thomas always has good ideas about what bait to use. Bill scans the hall. He spies Thomas but Martha is already pulling him down the aisle and he follows rather than attract more attention towards them. But his face is drawn, and if Martha would take time to notice, she would see the little lines of annoyance playing across his forehead.

They end up beside Joanie Bateson. Bill can't understand it. Of all people, Joanie Bateson. Non-stop-talking — Mrs. Verbal Diarrhea 1983, and Martha sits beside her. Bill pokes at his shrimp cocktail.

By eight o'clock the "tired" Martha has kicked off her high heels and is dancing with anyone who will ask her. It's as if the party has charged her batteries.

Martha: Come on Bill, let's have a dance. A nice slow sexy one.
Bill: (Blushing, giving her a disparaging look.)
         Martha, be still.

(But Martha pulls him to his feet. The wine has made Martha affectionate. She holds Bill close to her and lets her hand trail over his buttocks.)

Bill: Martha, if you don't behave I'm going to sit down.

(He puts her hand on his shoulders. He'd love to whisper sweet promises in her ear, but he is tired and getting grumpy. He feels guilty about his poor mood. He tries to perk up.)

Martha: There, I told you you'd feel better once you dance. You need to get your adrenalin going. Once I get started I could just dance all night.

(Martha twirls happily around the floor, weaving around Bill, who only smiles, shaking his head slightly.)

Finally Bill settles down with a drink next to Thomas. They find a quiet cubbyhole behind several palm trees and trade fishing secrets. Mercifully an hour slips by and Bill feels fairly confident that he can now talk Martha into going home. When he finds her she is talking to Joanie Bateson.

Martha: And when Bill's mother gave the farm to Bill's younger brother, well, we just about died. Bill will never forgive her. I mean, after all the years Bill put in. . . .
Bill: Martha, I'm going home.

(The voice is sharp. Angry. Martha decides not to argue.)

The drive home is uncomfortable. Neither speaks. Martha can't understand why Bill is so upset. She has a few ideas. On the edges of her mind she knows, but she is almost deciding to be defensive.

Martha: (Complaining, hoping to get Bill off track)
         We're always the first to go home.
Bill: (Holding back his anger.)
         I don't want to talk about it.
Martha: You never want to talk about anything. Tell me why you are mad. Are you mad? Just how are you feeling anyway?
Bill: We'll discuss it tomorrow.
Martha: (Voice rising as an old point of contention surfaces.)
         Tomorrow. Tomorrow! We always have to talk about it tomorrow. I want to talk about it now.
(Softly)
         I won't be able to sleep unless we talk about it, Bill.
Bill: I need to think about it. Sort it out. I'll explain it to you on Sunday. I'll think about it tomorrow. It's hard to explain. I guess I just don't trust people the way you do. I'm doing

fishing tomorrow. And *please*, for God's sake don't discuss it with Sally before we talk. I will think about it. I promise. Why don't you use your own noggin' instead of getting ideas from half the old maids in Prince Albert? It's our problem. Ok? I'll sort it out while I'm fishing.

Martha: (Glad to be on a friendly level)
Fishing. Is that what you and Thomas were hiding out to talk about.

(She laughs.)

Bill: (A bit offended)
We weren't hiding — we were talking about some new hooks Thomas has been making. Out of his wife's feather hats.

(He laughs.)

Martha: Where are you going?
Bill: Just up the coast. Think I'll take the tent. Spend the night.
Martha: Oh, I'd love that.
Bill: (A little uncomfortable)
I . . . uh, I thought I'd go by myself.
Martha: Oh.
Bill: I'd just like to be on my own.
Martha: Yeah. Ok.

(Later that night in bed)

Martha: Are you mad at me?
Bill: No, honey. I just don't like parties.
Martha: I didn't mean about the party. Guess I'd forgotten about that. I mean . . . did I do something wrong?
Bill: Wrong?
Martha: Well, the last time we went fishing, I lost that big one, getting so excited, almost jumping out of the boat.
Bill: Silly. No. That was funny. God, you should have seen yourself.

(Silence)

Martha: Then why don't you want to take me?
Bill: It's not that I don't want to take you. It's just that I'd like to be on my own. By myself. Ya know? To really get everything clear.
Martha: (Almost in tears)
Yeah. I know.

But she doesn't. Martha is an extravert. She doesn't understand, just as her introverted husband doesn't. Knowing the point of view behind each other's actions might have saved a lot of frustration and prevented many hurt feelings.

An examination of the communication may clarify how both parties could benefit from an understanding of each other's typologies.

An extraverted wife, Martha, returns home from a day's nursing. She is tired. Her introverted husband, Bill, is tired, too. It has been a long week and he is looking forward to being away from the office for a few days.

Martha: Tired, whew, I'm beat.
(She flops into a chair and puts her feet onto the ottoman. She groans.)
Bill: Me, too.
(He sits on the floor beside his wife and rubs her aching feet affectionately.)
            Guess we won't have to go to the banquet tonight — thank God.
(Martha takes her foot away. She sits up straight.)
Martha: The party, I forgot.
(She jumps up, rushing towards the bathroom.)
            I have to set my hair.
Bill: But you said you were beat.
(He looks baffled.)
Martha: (Already washing her hair)
            Watcha say?
Bill: I'm tired.
(He isn't sure why, but he's a bit angry.)
Martha: You'll feel better once we get there.
(Bill throws Martha a disparaging glance and switches on the TV. He is silent.)

The banquet does not go well. They come in one half hour late (Martha's hair not being dry on time) and have to trip through the entire banquet hall to find seats. Martha loves it. She "hi's" and hugs everyone in sight. These are her friends and although she sees them at work every day she seems delighted to see them again. Bill does not. He mumbles a few hellos and tries to get out of the limelight as fast as possible.

He wishes his wife would stop her endless greetings and he hopes he can find a seat near Thomas who loves to fish, as Bill does. Thomas always has good ideas about what bait to use. Bill scans the hall. He spies Thomas but Martha is already pulling him down the aisle and he follows rather than attract more attention towards them. But his face is drawn, and if Martha would take time to notice, she would see the little lines of annoyance playing across his forehead.

They end up beside Joanie Bateson. Bill can't understand it. Of all people, Joanie Bateson. Non-stop-talking — Mrs. Verbal Diarrhea 1983, and Martha sits beside her. Bill pokes at his shrimp cocktail.

Although Martha is genuinely tired the thought of a party perks her up. An extravert gets energy from interacting with other people. It's as though a battery charger had just been applied to the extravert's system. This is hard for an introvert to understand, because the opposite is true for him. If faced with a large group of people, his plug gets pulled, all energy draining into the chair. A tired introvert needs to get away by himself, to collect his thoughts, and recharge his batteries in quiet, private territory. Bill is angry at Martha's lack of understanding, and her sudden action-oriented attitude. She rushes about getting ready. He, reflective, feeling pushed into something he does not enjoy, hides in the television set.

Martha does not mind being late. She loves being the centre of attention. She does not mind being interrupted, or interrupting others. Being "fashionably" late is part of the fun.

If Bill has to endure a party involving a large group of people, he can tolerate it better if he can select someone he knows well and with whom he shares a common interest. This is a more tolerable interaction.

Bill is irritated and tired when having to tolerate a relative stranger whom he does not admire and whom he considers to be very "talkative." Had Joanie been less disagreeable in Bill's eyes, he might have enjoyed "hiding" in the sweep of her and his wife's extraversion.

By eight o'clock the "tired" Martha has kicked off her high heels and is dancing with anyone who will ask her. It's as if the party has charged her batteries.

Martha: Come on Bill, let's have a dance. A nice slow sexy one.

Bill: *(Blushing, giving her a disparaging look.)*
Martha, be still.

(But Martha pulls him to his feet. The wine has made Martha affectionate. She holds Bill close to her and lets her hand trail over his buttocks.)

Bill: Martha, if you don't behave I'm going to sit down.

(He puts her hand on his shoulders. He'd love to whisper sweet promises in her ear, but he is tired and getting grumpy. He feels guilty about his poor mood. He tries to perk up.)

Bill continues to fatigue; Martha to energize. To add insult to injury Martha does become quite "familiar." Extraverts can be very open and free with emotions. Introverts prefer to be private. Bill enjoys Martha's affection, almost feels guilty about rejecting it. However, he cannot abide the public display of affection. He feels embarrassed, conspicuous, vulnerable. What extraverts find hard to realize is that introverts NEVER quite trust their environment.

Martha: There, I told you you'd feel better once you dance. You need to get your adrenalin going. Once I get started I could just dance all night.

(Martha twirls happily around the floor, weaving around Bill, who only smiles, shaking his head slightly.)

Martha is enjoying herself so much, she assumes Bill is feeling the same way. She has lost her fatigue and does not notice his has increased.

Finally Bill settles down with a drink next to Thomas. They find a quiet cubbyhole behind several palm trees and trade fishing secrets. Mercifully an hour slips by and Bill feels fairly confident that he can now talk Martha into going home.

In desperation Bill seeks a refuge. Thomas, himself an introvert, shares his need for a place in which they can escape, happily discussing something they both care about – fishing.

When he finds her she is talking to Joanie Bateson.

Martha: And when Bill's mother gave the farm to Bill's younger brother, well, we just about died. Bill will never forgive her. I mean, after all the years Bill put in. . . .

Bill: Martha, I'm going home.

(The voice is sharp. Angry. Martha decides not to argue.)

This interaction is pleasant for both introverts. However, the respite is short-lived. Bill returns to find Martha discussing his private affairs with the town gossip. It is too much. If Bill was upset with Martha's being overly affectionate in public, he is furious about this betrayal. The risk involved is unbearable. He cannot understand Martha's foolishness, and, to his view, cruel actions, any more than she can fully imagine his anger. She often feels that she has made a mistake. She often feels angry at herself for getting carried away with a story. Often she has said far more than she had intended. She seems to get started and then seems unable to stop.

If she had taken time to think she wouldn't have told Joanie about Bill's mother — it just seemed to pop out of her mouth. Now she is sorry, but it is too late. It is just that she trusts everyone — even that silly Joanie Bateson. Although Martha understands this and feels guilty, she cannot understand the depth of Bill's intolerance for what she has done. She'd like to understand. She is right that she is missing something — but it is not what she thinks. Martha seeks things in the environment to explain Bill's moods, assuming it is things from WITHOUT that upset him, as they do her. Rather it is his INNER world which troubles him, his introverted attitude which causes him to need a respite from the environment, not a change in it.

If Bill is forced to deal directly with his environment and things which trouble him, then he needs time to reflect on it before discussing it with someone else. His extraverted wife, quite in contrast, not only does not need time to reflect, but needs immediate

The drive home is uncomfortable. Neither speaks. Martha can't understand why Bill is so upset. She has a few ideas. On the edges of her mind she knows, but she is almost deciding to be defensive.

Martha:	(Complaining, hoping to get Bill off track)
	We're always the first to go home.
Bill:	(Holding back his anger.)
	I don't want to talk about it.
Martha:	You never want to talk about anything. Tell me why you are mad. Are you mad? Just how are you feeling anyway?
Bill:	We'll discuss it tomorrow.
Martha:	(Voice rising as an old point of contention surfaces.)
	Tomorrow. Tomorrow! We always have to talk about it tomorrow. I want to talk about it now.
(Softly)	
	I won't be able to sleep unless we talk about it, Bill.
Bill:	I need to think about it. Sort it out. I'll explain it to you on Sunday. I'll think about it tomorrow. It's hard to explain. I guess I just don't trust people the way you do. I'm doing fishing tomorrow. And please, for God's sake don't discuss it with Sally before we talk. I will think about it. I promise. Why don't you use your own noggin' instead of getting ideas from half the old maids in Prince Albert? It's our problem. Ok? I'll sort it out while I'm fishing.

Martha: (Glad to be on a friendly level)
           Fishing. Is that what you and Thomas
           were hiding out to talk about.
(She laughs.)
Bill: (A bit offended)
           We weren't hiding — we were talking
           about some new hooks Thomas has
           been making. Out of his wife's feather
           hats.
(He laughs.)

action. Martha discovers what she knows about a thing by talking about it. Reflecting to her means brooding, it tends to depress her. Bill must win this point of dispute. Although Martha prefers to discuss the issue now, she *will be able to* discuss it later. Bill *cannot* discuss it now. He needs time to get his thoughts together. If this does not happen Martha may well "win" the argument, but she will never know Bill's true thoughts on the matter and little will be accomplished in strengthening their relationship. It is clear both parties care very much for one another. Understanding one another would allow Martha to give Bill the time he needs without her feeling rejected or thinking Bill is being stubborn. Bill, too, could take the time to be reflective without feeling guilty.

Martha, at this point, must assume the responsibility to resist another urge so common to the extravert — that of turning to another for advice. Discouraged by Bill's refusal to discuss the matter, Martha may naturally turn to a friend, telling the tale, asking "What should I do?" There is nothing wrong with this. However, if Martha's main motive is to improve communication with Bill, then she risks offending him on two counts. First, Bill is very private and deeply resents "outsiders" knowing about his family troubles. This is true even of a trusted family friend. Extraverts have a hard time realizing the degree to which this is ture. Second, Bill resents Martha's "wishy-washy" attitude. Bill wishes Martha could make up her own mind. It seems she changes her opinion with every person she talks to. This really disturbs his internal system. He cannot value such action. He considers it weak, one of Martha's worst faults. He does not understand that the wonderful caring and ability to respond to his needs that Martha so often displays in other circumstances grows from the same source as this "wishy-washiness" does. The introvert experiences a very subjective, internal source of motivation. The introvert must listen, essentially, to himself. Martha may see this as a stubborn or selfish streak. It is not. It can be a great source of strength and independence and should be regarded as that. Extraverts need to please others, to check out others' ideas and expectations, to serve an external source of motivation. In contrast to the introverted independence, this can be delightful and charming and facilitative; both must be seen as they are, to be appreciated.

Martha:	Where are you going?
Bill:	Just up the coast. Think I'll take the tent. Spend the night.
Martha:	Oh, I'd love that.
Bill:	(A little uncomfortable) I . . . uh, I thought I'd go by myself.
Martha:	Oh.
Bill:	I'd just like to be on my own.
Martha:	Yeah. Ok.

And now comes one of the most difficult things for the truly extraverted person to understand — that when an introvert is saying, "I want to be alone," he means only that. An extravert hears, "I don't want to be with you," and wonders why.

(Later that night in bed)

Martha: Are you mad at me?

Bill: No, honey. I just don't like parties.

Martha: I didn't mean about the party. Guess
          I'd forgotten about that. I mean . . .
          did I do something wrong?

Bill: Wrong?

Martha: Well, the last time we went fishing, I
          lost that big one, getting so excited,
          almost jumping out of the boat.

Bill: Silly. No. That was funny. God, you
          should have seen yourself.

(Silence)

Martha: Then why don't you want to take
          me?

Bill: It's not that I don't want to take you.
          It's just that I'd like to be on my own.
          By myself. Ya know? To really get
          everything clear.

Martha: (Almost in tears)
          Yeah. I know.

Martha clearly does not hear what Bill has said. She searches herself for fault. She seeks an answer in the external environment. True to her extraverted nature she:

— wants to be part of the activity
— feels rejected when she is not
— cannot understand his need to be alone on what could be such a "chance" to get together
— wants to please
— searches for reasons in things OUTSIDE Bill's mind.

The answer, of course, is in Bill's mind. Because he truly does care about what's happening, he insists on the time to reflect, to gather his energy so that perhaps he and Martha can clear up the disputes haunting them and understood by neither of them.

The tragedy is that unless they can see things "through one another's eyes," it is difficult to trust what is happening. Martha does not see Bill's act as being one of caring in any sense. She will brood and feel rejected during his absence. This will not put her in a good frame of mind for discussion upon his return.

Understanding of both types might have allowed Bill to include Martha in the overall trip, and to assure her of his careful, caring consideration of their dispute. She, aware of his need to reflect, could accept the invitation happily, promising him hours of peaceful solitary fishing time during their trip — wise compromise being a soothing peacemaker.

"What Is It? What Could It Be?"

Sensing and Intuition Try to Understand One Another

Claudia and James are having a problem. They think it might be the fact that they have been married for sixteen years. James is worried that Claudia doesn't care about him any more. She says she does, but actions speak louder than words, and this is about the hundredth time he's complained. . . .

James: You're never interested in things I like to do. You seldom even sit still long enough to watch a TV show I like, or to work on a jigsaw puzzle with me.

Claudia: (Sincerely)
           But I am interested, I love going to movies with you, lots of things, I just get a bit restless sometimes.

James: Restless! you get flighty. Flighty is what you get. Hell, you can't do one thing for more than five minutes. Look at the spare room. You have a dress half sewn, a pair of pants all ready except for the hem, and enough material to outfit half of Vancouver. Moreover, there's that set of oil paints you *had* to have, that old couch you've been meaning to recover all winter and. . . .

(The old hurt is back and Claudia turns cruel.)

Claudia: And you sure don't mind when you get a handmade silk shirt, do you? Or when I fix up the living room and everyone thinks we hired a fancy interior decorator to do it! You sure wouldn't have the imagination, would you. You never think of anything. Dullsville man! Complain, nag, that's you.

James: (Quick to retaliate, equally hurt)
           Never think, ay? Well who remembered your mother's birthday? You may be smart when it comes to reading books, lady. But boy when it comes to living — everyday living — you are dumb. D.U.M.B. dumb. I have never seen anybody with so little common sense. Sometimes you do the dumbest things. Like getting lost on the way to Jody's school and showing up an hour late for your meeting with her teacher. If I know you, you even left your office a half hour late to begin with. If you REALLY CARED. . . .''

(James lets the words hang in the air.)

Claudia: (Picks up on the theme that matters, and speaks earnestly.)
           And if you REALLY CARED you'd understand and accept the fact that I did want to be there on time. I just got lost. Dammit,

lost! Anyway if you *really cared* you'd be more interested in why I had to go, if I got there on time. . . .

(Jody pipes in, not letting her mother hypothesize. She too was disturbed by her mother's lateness.)

Jody: Dad's right. Mom. It is embarrassing when you're late. Once you even forgot completely. How can it be important when you do that?

(Claudia is silenced. Neither husband nor child understand her. Defeated, she leaves the room. It takes three days of quiet hurting before the family can return to normal interacting.)

Jody: Boy, that was easy. Thanks for helping me, Dad, you're better than an encyclopedia.

James: (Proudly)
          Facts always were my good point. Dates, names, they just stick in the old noggin. Any time, Jody, any time.

Claudia: Did you finish all your homework?

Jody: Yeah — all my history, except for a couple of dumb questions at the end.

Claudia: Oh. Like. . . ?

Jody: Just dumb ones, Mom. The teacher always sticks 'em on the end. They don't make any difference. There's no real answer. I could write any old thing.

Claudia: (Knowing her daughter well)
          Let's hear one.

Jody: (Reluctantly, not valuing this transaction, she reads in a sing-song voice.)
          "What might have happened if Louis Riel had not been killed?"

Claudia: That's an interesting thought.

Jody: But it's silly. He *was* killed. Those are the facts. He was.

Claudia: (Knowing her daughter very well)
          Jody, what facts do you have that might give you some good clues as to what would have happened? Rewrite history based on those facts.

(Jody thinks hard, and her face lights up. She starts writing. Claudia returns to the kitchen, having momentarily redeemed herself.)

  (The next day Claudia and Jody are shopping.)

Claudia: Help me pick out a book for your father. He needs a little "pick me up." Maybe this *Charcoal Burners* by Susan Musgrave.

Jody: Mom, she writes poetry. Dad hates poetry.

Claudia: No, this is a novel. (Her voice trails off.)

Jody: Here, Mom.

(She hands her mother *Everything You Ever Wanted to Know About Volkswagens*.)

And I'll get this?
(It is a question. She holds *T.V. Trivia 1981*.)
(Claudia walks to the counter. She is carrying an anthology of poetry. She purchases all three.)

Jody: (Excited, coaxing)
           Can we go on a picnic? Let's get some hot dogs.
Claudia: We'll see.
Jody: (Trying to force the issue)
           Mom.
Claudia: (Busy examining some material)
           I said, "we'll see." Probably.
Jody: (Disappointed)
           You said that last week.
Claudia: (Turning to her daughter)
           I did, didn't I?
(Jody looks up beseechingly)
Claudia: Ok. Tomorrow is Sunday. We'll go. Let's go get some goodies.
(They go off together, a team.)
Jody: Mom, do you think I should ask Michael to come?
Claudia: Was Tuesday the last time you saw him?
Jody: Yeah, really. Well, we said "hi" at school a couple of times.
           But watcha' really think, Mom. Should I? What if he says no.
           I'll die.
Claudia: He sure didn't look like he'd say no on Tuesday. I'd lay my
           money on his loving to come. Sure, ask him.
Jody: (Glowing)
           Mom, you're a genius.
(At the picnic)
Michael: Mrs. Thompson, this is wonderful. Hazelnut Torte is my favorite
           dessert. Hardly anyone ever makes it. How'd you know?
Claudia: Just a wizard. I guess.
James: (Laughing, reading his book on Volkswagens)
           She is. It's true. A wizard.
Claudia: (Hugging Jody)
           Well, sometimes I get a little help from my friends.
Jody: But Mom, I didn't know Michael liked Hazelnut Torte. How
           did you?
Claudia: I'm not sure. Just a hunch, I guess. . . .

Claudia and James are having a problem. They think it might be the fact that they have been married for sixteen years. James is worried that Claudia doesn't care about him any more. She says she does, but actions speak louder than words, and this is about the hundredth time he's complained. . . .

James: *You're never interested in things I like to do. You seldom even sit still long enough to watch a TV show I like, or to work on a jigsaw puzzle with me.*

Claudia: *(Sincerely)*
But I am interested, I love going to movies with you, lots of things, I just get a bit restless sometimes.

James: *Restless! you get flighty. Flighty is what you get. Hell, you can't do one thing for more than five minutes. Look at the spare room. You have a dress half sewn, a pair of pants all ready except for the hem, and enough material to outfit half of Vancouver. Moreover, there's that set of oil paints you had to have, that old couch you've been meaning to recover all winter and. . . .*

(The old hurt is back and Claudia turns cruel.)
Claudia: *And you sure don't mind when you get a handmade silk shirt, do you? Or when I fix up the living room and everyone thinks we hired a fancy interior decorator to do it! You sure wouldn't have the imagination, would you. You never think of anything. Dullsville man! Complain, nag, that's you.*

James, being a sensing type, enjoys factual, here-and-now, simple activities such as watching TV or playing crossword puzzles, whereas Claudia finds such activities don't sutain her interest. In fact, they drain her energies.

James interprets this as lack of caring and so he attacks Claudia for what he sees as her extreme flightiness. It is the sensing person's typology to be stable, to be involved in one activity at a time. The intuitive, on the other hand, enjoys working on several projects simultaneously. This does not mean Claudia will not complete her tasks. Her need to find closure will depend on whether or not she is a judging or a perceiving type. *Real* trouble in this area occurs when a sensing judging type is trying to regulate the activities of an intuitive perceiving type.

Claudia is fairly secure in the knowledge that although she does undertake a variety of projects, her creative abilities allow her to achieve some excellent results. James, for all his practical nature, does not have this imaginative drive. Having been attacked for something she actually does well, Claudia turns the ridicule James' way. Having been married long, these two are quite aware of one another's strengths and weaknesses, of the very things which make them a complementary team. But right now they are preoccupied with accusing and

James: (Quick to retaliate, equally hurt)
            Never think, ay? Well who
            remembered your mother's birthday?
            You may be smart when it comes to
            reading books, lady. But boy when it
            comes to living — everyday living —
            you are dumb. D.U.M.B. dumb. I
            have never seen anybody with so little
            common sense. Sometimes you do the
            dumbest things. Like getting lost on
            the way to Jody's school and showing
            up an hour late for your meeting with
            her teacher. If I know you, you even
            left your office a half hour late to
            begin with. If you REALLY
            CARED. . . ."
(James lets the words hang in the air.)

Claudia: (Picks up on the theme that matters,
            and speaks earnestly.)
            And if you REALLY CARED you'd
            understand and accept the fact that I
            did want to be there on time. I just
            got lost. Dammit, lost! Anyway if you
            really cared you'd be more interested
            in why I had to go, if I got there on
            time. . . .
(Jody pipes in, not letting her mother
hypothesize. She too was disturbed by her
mother's lateness.)

Jody: Dad's right. Mom. It is embarrassing
            when you're late. Once you even
            forgot completely. How can it be im-
            portant when you do that?

being defensive. Indeed, as good as Claudia is at being creative — one of the gifts naturally afforded the intuitive — she is poor at paying attention to details. Herein lies the sensing type's strength. It is quite easy for James to remember birthdays, appointments, phone numbers, addresses, dates in history, facts important and even unimportant. Claudia sometimes has difficulty with the important details — like remembering an appointment with her daughter's teacher. James' accusation "if you really cared" is especially hurting and quite untrue. If Claudia is a feeling type, she will be especially bothered by her "scatterbrain" tendencies. She knows that being late or even forgetting appointments makes it appear that she does not value the people or situation — involved. And this is the way most people interpret her actions. What would be more helpful for everybody is to understand Claudia's difficulty and to help her with subtle reminders. It would be most useful for Claudia if she herself recognized that her sensing shadow was causing this trouble. Instead of feeling guilty and wondering "what is wrong with me," she could turn to her sensing husband and daughter for help. She could also incorporate in her life-style such reminders as daily journals, large calendars with appointments and important dates recorded on them. Instead of wasting negative energy on blame and frustration, intuitive types are wise to find creative means of

(Claudia is silenced. Neither husband nor child understand her. Defeated, she leaves the room. It takes three days of quiet hurting before the family can return to normal interacting.)

Jody:	*Boy, that was easy. Thanks for helping me, Dad, you're better than an encyclopedia.*
James:	*(Proudly)*
	Facts always were my good point. Dates, names, they just stick in the old noggin. Any time, Jody, any time.
Claudia:	*Did you finish all your homework?*
Jody:	*Yeah — all my history, except for a couple of dumb questions at the end.*
Claudia:	*Oh. Like. . . ?*
Jody:	*Just dumb ones, Mom. The teacher always sticks 'em on the end. They don't make any difference. There's no real answer. I could write any old thing.*
Claudia:	*(Knowing her daughter well)*
	Let's hear one.
Jody:	*(Reluctantly, not valuing this transaction, she reads in a singsong voice.)*
	"What might have happened if Louis Riel had not been killed?"
Claudia:	*That's an interesting thought.*
Jody:	*But it's silly. He was killed. Those are the facts. He was.*
Claudia:	*(Knowing her daughter very well)*
	Jody, what facts do you have that might give you some good clues as to what would have happened? Rewrite history based on those facts.

(Jody thinks hard, and her face lights up. She starts writing. Claudia returns to the kitchen, having momentarily redeemed herself.)

(The next day Claudia and Jody are shopping.)

Claudia:	*Help me pick out a book for your father. He needs a little "pick me up." Maybe this* Charcoal Burners *by Susan Musgrave.*
Jody:	*Mom, she writes poetry. Dad hates poetry.*

compensating for their weak areas.

James is at his best in helping Jody with her homework because of the sensing type's love of facts. Both Jody and her father find the activity stimulating, and easy. What Jody will have a natural tendency to avoid is questions dealing with possibilities. This stems from her here-and-now, realistic orientation. A sensing type must be *taught* to value future-oriented, analytic, or imaginative questions. Claudia finds these questions challenging, as would most intuitives. What is boring to one type is exciting to the other. However, Claudia knows the key to her daughter's interest and uses Jody's strength to allow her to develop her weaker function by asking, "What FACTS do you have. . . ?" and Jody is on her way. This is wise use of knowledge of perception patterns that Claudia has somehow intuitively discovered. Often intuitive types are "aware" of typology without even having it explained to them. Sensing types, on the other hand, want plenty of examples and some pretty hard data to prove that typology as a system really exists.

On the shopping spree Claudia is not choosing a gift for James based on what she knows about him rather she chooses a book that appeals to her intuitive nature. Intuitives love novels, books of

Claudia: No, this is a novel. (Her voice trails off.)

Jody: Here, Mom.

(She hands her mother Everything You Ever Wanted to Know About Volkswagens.)
      And I'll get this?

(It is a question. She holds T.V. Trivia 1981.)

(Claudia walks to the counter. She is carrying an anthology of poetry. She purchases all three.)

Jody: (Excited, coaxing)
      Can we go on a picnic? Let's get some hot dogs.

Claudia: We'll see.

Jody: (Trying to force the issue)
      Mom.

Claudia: (Busy examining some material)
      I said, "we'll see." Probably.

Jody: (Disappointed)
      You said that last week.

Claudia: (Turning to her daughter)
      I did, didn't I?

(Jody looks up beseechingly)

Claudia: Ok. Tomorrow is Sunday. We'll go. Let's go get some goodies.

(They go off together, a team.)

Jody: Mom, do you think I should ask Michael to come?

Claudia: Was Tuesday the last time you saw him?

Jody: Yeah, really. Well, we said "hi" at school a couple of times. But watcha' really think, Mom. Should I? What if he says no. I'll die.

Claudia: He sure didn't look like he'd say no on Tuesday. I'd lay my money on his loving to come. Sure, ask him.

Jody: (Glowing)
      Mom, you're a genius.

(At the picnic)

Michael: Mrs. Thompson, this is wonderful. Hazelnut Torte is my favorite dessert. Hardly anyone ever makes it. How'd you know?

Claudia: Just a wizard. I guess.

James: (Laughing, reading his book on Volkswagens)
      She is. It's true. A wizard.

Claudia: (Hugging Jody)
      Well, sometimes I get a little help from my friends.

Jody: But Mom, I didn't know Michael liked Hazelnut Torte. How did you?

Claudia: I'm not sure. Just a hunch, I guess. . . .

poetry, of philosophy. Sensing types are far more practical. They want books about real things. Jody knows this and chooses for her father.

When the topic of picnic-going arises, Jody is excited. She loves to do things. But her needs are immediate. Delay means negation. This is especially true of sensing perceiving children. "Now" seems to be their favorite word.

And so Claudia gives in. Feeling good, Jody decides to use her mother's strength, her great ability of somehow "just knowing" what other people are thinking. This knack enjoyed by intuitives seems to baffle sensing types who need more obvious data. Despite their ability to notice details, sensing types do not "read between the lines" or "add up tiny clues" as do intuitives. Sensing types are so awed by this ability of the intuitive, they often call it magic or ESP.

Even when Claudia is questioned about her ability to know things like Michael's favorite dessert, she can't explain it. An intuitive often is unaware of where she gleaned her knowledge. Somehow she picks up clues, but in her scanning process she often refers to her knowledge source as "just a hunch."

"Please Understand Me"

A Thinking Type Interacts with Several Feeling Types

Ted teaches science at Smithson High. His students regard him as a good teacher. And he is. He can explain ideas very clearly. He is dedicated to learning, taking endless pains to help his students in any way he can, but some days. . . .

Ted: Carol, you haven't finished your experiment.
Carol: Sorry.
Ted: It's the second time this week.
Carol: I'll catch up next week, Mr. Thompson.
Ted: I'll be staying after school today. I'll help you.
Carol: I kinda got something on my mind, Mr. Thompson, I'd rather. . . .
Ted: If you get too far behind it will just discourage you. You'd better stay.
(Having dealt fairly and helpfully with Carol, Ted moves on to Alvin, a sensitive young man who, despite his strong desire to please the teacher, is often careless with his experiments.)
Ted: Good work, Alvin. Your measurements were very precise.
(Alvin smiles, thrilled with having pleased the teacher.)
Ted: To improve what you are doing, next time, write down your observations as they occur, rather than relying on your memory.
(Ted laughs good humoredly.)
          Because as we all know, it has a tendency to fail you at times.
(Always quick to show emotion, Alvin drops his head to hide his shame. He blushes; the students around the table join in the laughter.)
    Ted does not notice the tears filling the boy's eyes as he moves on. As Ted leaves the building he meets the principal and hears words that have become quite familiar to them both.

Principal: Keep up the great work.
Ted: (Uneasily) Thanks, Ok. . . . good night.
(He leaves. He arrives home before his wife Ann. She comes in almost an hour late. She is irritable. She has been irritable for almost a week.)
Ted: You're late. Keep them in for detention?
Ann: (Throwing her bundle of books on the desk.)
           Yes.
Ted: They give you a hard time?
Ann: Yes.
(Ann is almost in tears.)

(Ted, glancing through the paper, looks up at his too quiet wife.)

Ted: What did they do?

Ann: (Her voice trembles.)
        Talked, yelled, threw paper airplanes, Mark told me to "cool it!"

Ted: What did you do?

Ann: I shouldn't be a teacher. I just don't have it.

Ted: What were you doing that Mark told you to "cool it!"?

Ann: I was trying to get him to finish his story. I was trying to teach the little sucker!

(Her voice is too shrill, too defensive.)

Ted: Probably you should've clamped down on him a month ago. You're so soft. If you had. . . .

Ann: (Abruptly uncomfortable)
        Shut up!

Ted: Hell, Ann, I was only. . . .

Ann: Well don't.

Ted: You know what's really bothering you.

Ann: Yes. Teaching. Housecleaning. Working. Cooking. Being tired.

Ted: Pal, that's what.

Ann: What?

Ted: Pal. You're worried about that dog again.

Ann: (Soft, almost in tears)
        I am. We've never left him.

Ted: A trip to Europe. The whole summer, our first holiday, and she's worried about what to do with a dog.

Ann: He's old.

Ted: My point exactly.

Ann: He'll hate it in a kennel.

Ted: Who else wants to take care of an old, deaf, loose-boweled cocker spaniel?

Ann: He'll miss us terribly. I wonder if my mother. . . .

Ted: Fly him all the way to your mother's? We sure can't afford it right now with the trip and all. Anyway, Ann, you know what we should do.

Ann: (Paling)
        What?

Ted: You know.

Ann: Ted, if you suggest, one more time, that. . . .

Ted: It would be best all round.

Ann: I've had that dog since I was a girl.

Ted: Be reasonable. It's just a dog.

(Silence)

Ted: For his own good.

(Silence)

Ted: He's going to get sicker and older. He's already deaf. He shits on the rug whenever he gets into any bones or garbage. It'll cost us a fortune anyway, you said yourself he'd hate it in the kennel.

(Ann glares at her husband. The phone rings. It is Ted's best friend, George. It is bad news. George's son has been killed in a motorcycle accident. George is a widower. He is wild with grief. He is confused, desperate.)

Ted: I don't know what to say, George. (Pause) It's awful. When did it happen. . . . George, just calm down now. . . . take it easy, pal. . . . George, why don't you talk to Ann.

(He turns the phone over to his wife.)

Ann: Oh, George, I am so sorry. There are no words to describe how you must be feeling. No one can really ever know. . . . Yes. . . . that's right. . . . oh yes. . . . Please George, let Ted go and pick you up. You should spend a few days with us. Just to be here around friends. . . . hush now. . . . Ted will be there in a few minutes.

(She motions for Ted to get going.)

And Ted leaves, knowing his wife will be able to comfort George, will know just the thing to say — though she hardly really knows George, she will be great. She always is in these situations. And Ted feels suddenly awkward and inadequate. He remembers the time his mother came to visit. How much she wanted him to tell her how much he loved her. How much she needed words to prove the obvious. He was her son. He was feeling the same in this situation, the same — guilty, frustrated, confused. And anguished. For his best friend, and the loss of this son. Ted wanted to cry. He drove carefully into George's driveway.

There's a lot of uneasiness in these interactions. Something is out of kilter. Something is missing the mark. Feelings are being hurt. A thinking person is feeling inadequate. An analysis of these transactions might show why. Whether you identify with Ann, Carol or Alvin, the feeling types, or Ted, the thinking type, doesn't really matter. What matters is that you understand the differences in point of view, for in understanding comes an eradication of the uneasiness.

Ted teaches science at Smithson High. His
students regard him as a good teacher. And he is.
He can explain ideas very clearly. He is dedicated
to learning, taking endless pains to help his
students in any way he can, but some days. . . .

Ted:	*Carol, you haven't finished your*
	experiment.
Carol:	*Sorry.*
Ted:	*It's the second time this week.*
Carol:	*I'll catch up next week, Mr.*
	Thompson.
Ted:	*I'll be staying after school today. I'll*
	help you.
Carol:	*I kinda got something on my mind,*
	Mr. Thompson, I'd rather. . . .
Ted:	*If you get too far behind it will just*
	discourage you. You'd better stay.

(Having dealt fairly and helpfully with Carol, Ted
moves on to Alvin, a sensitive young man who,
despite his strong desire to please the teacher, is
often careless with his experiments.)

It is the nature of a thinking-type person to analyse the facts in a rather clinical, objective way. Carol obviously has something on her mind, she is not ready to work this week. Instead of trying to pursue what's bothering Carol, or simply trusting her, Ted insists on "helping" her. It is logical that if she gets farther behind she will feel worse. Ted applies this logic and supplies a solution. And it may get the experiments done. But, Ted misses a chance to understand Carol, to trust her, to listen to her. *If* Carol is a feeling type, she will resent this. If she is a thinking type, she will probably appreciate Ted's efforts more because she will not be hurt by the parts of the interaction he tends to ignore. Understanding that Ted is a thinking type will help Carol not to be as frustrated and hurt by Ted's approach. Ted's understanding of his own preferences may allow him to tune in more carefully to Carol's feelings. It would become a rational thing to do — using his *best function*, thinking, he can analyse feelings as part of his data and make a decision based on all the facts. Awareness does not suggest that one works *against* oneself. The wise person can use his own strength (in this case, thinking) to help to accommodate his shadow, or weaker function (in this case, feeling).

Often the thinking-type person believes the best gift he can give someone is to criticize what the

Ted: *Good work, Alvin. Your*
             measurements were very precise.
(Alvin smiles, thrilled with having pleased the
teacher.)
Ted: *To improve what you are doing, next*
             time, write down your observations as
             they occur, rather than relying on
             your memory.
(Ted laughs good humoredly.)
             Because as we all know, it has a
             tendency to fail you at times.
(Always quick to show emotion, Alvin drops his
head to hide his shame. He blushes; the students
around the table join in the laughter.)
    Ted does not notice the tears filling the boy's
eyes as he moves on.

person does. His criticism, like his praise, is very precise. And if the criticism is going to another thinking type person, then it is quite acceptable, is indeed considered very useful. However, if the criticism is going to a feeling-type person, it is not so well received. Alvin is a feeling-type student. He likes to please his teacher. He is very happy when Ted praises him. The happiness is short-lived. It disappears at the criticism. Although Ted was careful to prescribe a specific solution for Alvin, Alvin is very sensitive about his poor work in this area. He is hurt by the laughter and considers his teacher cruel. He does not hear the caring in the suggestion. He hears the criticism, the ridicule. He does not appreciate his teacher's sense of humor. (A "cruel" sense of humor is a common complaint of feeling types when speaking of thinking types.) Alvin would probably have done much better work next time if Ted had stopped at the comment, "Good work, Alvin, your measurements were very precise." *Despite* the fact that Ted's criticism was very concrete and directive, it will probably not be accepted by Alvin. If you are a feeling type you will understand this very easily.

If you are a thinking type you will find it hard to believe. Just as Alvin does not benefit from criticism, Ted seems not to value praise, especially general praise too often given. Ted's principal's

As Ted leaves the building he meets the principal
and hears words that have become quite familiar
to them both.

Principal: *Keep up the great work.*
Ted: *(Uneasily) Thanks, Ok. . . . good*
             night.

general "Keep up the great work" does not thrill Ted too much. The principal, a feeling type, says it to everyone. He is always encouraging. "Big deal," thinks Ted, "it would be a lot more useful if the principal would spend more time in the classroom observing. Then he could tell me specifically what is good and what isn't." This analysis, and the specific praise and criticism which would accompany it, would be highly prized by the thinking type. It would have to be handled very carefully for the feeling-type teacher.

Analysis. Analysis. There Ted goes again offering his best process. He is trying desperately to help his wife. He sees her distress and so he tries to analyse its causes, so that she can find a logical solution to her discomfort. Perhaps she can avoid its being repeated. But Ann is not ready for this clinical and (she feels) very critical approach. She wishes she had not even trusted her husband with the truth. She is distraught over the many times he has let her down, not understood her. She wants his support, his empathy, not his brilliant ideas. She wants a walk in the park, a back rub, a dinner out. She does not want a lecture on "how to be a better teacher." If, instead of being hurt by her husband's approach, she understood it, things might have turned out differently. Instead of saying "shut up," Ann might have been able to say, "I appreciate your trying to figure this out for

(He leaves. He arrives home before his wife Ann. She comes in almost an hour late. She is irritable. She has been irritable for almost a week.)

Ted: You're late. Keep them in for detention?
Ann: *(Throwing her bundle of books on the desk.)*
Yes.
Ted: They give you a hard time?
Ann: Yes.
(Ann is almost in tears.)
(Ted, glancing through the paper, looks up at his too quiet wife.)
Ted: What did they do?
Ann: *(Her voice trembles.)*
Talked, yelled, threw paper airplanes, Mark told me to "cool it!"
Ted: What did you do?
Ann: I shouldn't be a teacher. I just don't have it.
Ted: What were you doing that Mark told you to "cool it!"?
Ann: I was trying to get him to finish his story. I was trying to teach the little sucker!
(Her voice is too shrill, too defensive.)
Ted: Probably you should've clamped down on him a month ago. You're so soft. If you had. . . .

Ann: *(Abruptly uncomfortable)*
Shut up!
Ted: Hell, Ann, I was only. . . .
Ann: Well don't.

me, Ted, but not today. I'm feeling too creepy to hear it. I just need some T.L.C." And probably she would have got it. Instead, both are hurting. The feeling type usually has to take the initiative in leading the thinking type in the feeling arenas. And why not? It is easier, more natural for the feeling type.

This next area is more difficult to solve. It involves logical, clinical, objective analysis of facts on one part; and a subjective values decision on the other. Ted can see all the *reasons* why the dog should be put to sleep. He would miss the dog, but he honestly sees the decision as clearly the correct one. Ann, on the other hand, *cannot* forgive his coldness. She hates this in her husband. Her value system simply does not allow her to put a pet to sleep. Yet another value says it is unfair to keep him in a kennel for two months. This is what is giving Ann so much trouble. Her value system is in conflict. When this happens to feeling types they suffer a great deal. They can become irritable, even ill. Teenagers suffer especially if they are feeling types and they are unclear about their values. Their whole centre is threatened. Change, such as divorce, moving, or loss of job, can also upset feeling types to the point of illness. Any time the value system is in jeopardy, so is the feeling type.

Ted:	You know what's really bothering you.
Ann:	Yes. Teaching. Housecleaning. Working. Cooking. Being tired.
Ted:	Pal, that's what.
Ann:	What?
Ted:	Pal. You're worried about that dog again.
Ann:	(Soft, almost in tears) I am. We've never left him.
Ted:	A trip to Europe. The whole summer, our first holiday, and she's worried about what to do with a dog.
Ann:	He's old.
Ted:	My point exactly.
Ann:	He'll hate it in a kennel.
Ted:	Who else wants to take care of an old, deaf, loose-boweled cocker spaniel?
Ann:	He'll miss us terribly. I wonder if my mother. . . .
Ted:	Fly him all the way to your mother's? We sure can't afford it right now with the trip and all. Anyway, Ann, you know what we should do.
Ann:	(Paling) What?
Ted:	You know.
Ann:	Ted, if you suggest, one more time, that. . . .
Ted:	It would be best all round.
Ann:	I've had that dog since I was a girl.
Ted:	Be reasonable. It's just a dog.
(Silence)	
Ted:	For his own good.
(Silence)	
Ted:	He's going to get sicker and older. He's already deaf. He shits on the rug whenever he gets into any bones or garbage. It'll cost us a fortune anyway, you said yourself he'd hate it in the kennel.

(Ann glares at her husband. The phone rings. It is Ted's best friend, George. It is bad news. George's son has been killed in a motorcycle accident. George is a widower. He is wild with grief. He is confused, desperate.)

Ted: I don't know what to say, George. (Pause) It's awful. When did it happen. . . . George, just calm down now. . . . take it easy, pal. . . . George, why don't you talk to Ann.

(He turns the phone over to his wife.)

Ann: Oh, George, I am so sorry. There are no words to describe how you must be feeling. No one can really ever know. . . . Yes. . . . that's right. . . . oh yes. . . . Please George, let Ted go and pick you up. You should spend a few days with us. Just to be here around friends. . . . hush now. . . . Ted will be there in a few minutes.

(She motions for Ted to get going.)

And Ted leaves, knowing his wife will be able to comfort George, will know just the thing to say — though she hardly really knows George, she will be great. She always is in these situations. And Ted feels suddenly awkward and inadequate. He remembers the time his mother came to visit. How much she wanted him to tell her how much he loved her. How much she needed words

Ted recognizes that in times when empathy is needed, his wife is the one to give it. Although Ann only knows George through phone calls and the odd staff party, she will be able to comfort him in time of crisis. It is as if the right thing to say just flows naturally from her. She can both get "inside" the other person and express her own feelings so clearly. Ted feels inadequate here. He even feels guilty that he does not know the right thing to say. He feels he has failed his friend. Or worse yet, he fears others will perceive him as being uncaring. And his fears are justified. Often that is the interpretation of the thinking type's lack of expression of feeling. It is not an accurate interpretation. We must be careful not to take a lack of *expression* of feeling to mean a lack of *feeling*. It is not that Ted feels no pain for the loss of his friend; it is that he finds it difficult to find the right words to talk about it. This is especially true if the thinking type is an introvert.

to prove the obvious. He was her son. He was feeling the same in this situation, the same — guilty, frustrated, confused. And anguished. For his best friend, and the loss of this son. Ted wanted to cry. He drove carefully into George's driveway.

As well, the thinking type expects that others will understand that feeling is behind his actions. "Why don't you ever tell me that you love me?" wails the feeling-type wife, who needs and appreciates verbal affirmation of affection. "But I live with you, don't I?" responds the astonished thinking-type husband. "Is that not proof enough?" Logically, perhaps.

This expression of emotion can be a very touchy issue amongst family members. It is wise to be quite open about the discomfort, so that misunderstandings are avoided. Often a thinking type will benefit from taking a course in human relations training. Dealing with feelings, then, can become part of his thinking process.

It is also very helpful for the feeling members of the family to try not to take the thinking-type person's critical and analytical attitude as a *personal* offence. Understanding it, rather, as a *way of* making decisions is far more beneficial for everyone concerned. It is also a good idea to encourage the thinking member of the family to offer advice and analysis in matters of business, in making major decisions. This will indicate a valuing of the process and it will be easier for the thinking type to accept it when he is asked to "reserve" his judgment for a more appropriate time.

"The Dominant Functions in Disharmony"

Judging versus Perceiving

When "definitely" meets "I'm not sure yet" it can mean trouble. Let's take a look. . . .

Sarah: I've always wanted to go to Greece.
Ann: There's so many places to choose from.
Sarah: Summer will be here before we know it.
Ann: I should get some brochures at the travel agency.
(One week later.)
Sarah: Did you get those brochures yet?
Ann: Sarah, it's only January.
Sarah: Only. Only. We have to book months in advance, Ann — You know that.
Ann: Ok. Ok. Don't get excited.
Sarah: I don't want it to turn out like our holiday to the Rockies.
Ann: It was wonderful!
Sarah: We had no hotel reservations. We had to spend two nights in the tent.
Ann: We got to see a whole herd of mountain goats.
Sarah: But we hadn't planned to sleep in a tent. We had planned to sleep in a luxury hotel. It was supposed to be a holiday.
Ann: It was a holiday.
Sarah: I just couldn't relax not knowing what would happen from one day to the next.
Ann: Some holiday — if every second has to be planned.
Sarah: Well, if we go to Greece — we HAVE to plan it — we won't just 'happen' to be carrying a tent in our purses, dearheart.
Ann: Quit saying Greece all the time as if we've decided.
(Three months later.)
Ann: Sarah, if you leave one more "list" for me I'll burn this apartment to the ground.
Sarah: Wow, aren't we in a good mood.
Ann: Well, it's bad enough at work — punch in, type this, file that, mail these, punch out, run for lunch, be at this meeting, meet this deadline, arrange for that flight, punch out, run for the bus. My life is an alarm clock of agendas and I come home to "Ann, please make sure you have done the following:
1. Check passport
2. Arrange for shots
3. Order back pack

4. Write to Tony
5. Make appointment for perm"
God, Sarah, put in a dime, turn the crank. Back off. I'll be
ready for this trip. Ease up — it's not even fun already.

Sarah: (Offended, confused)
I'm only trying to help.

Ann: Do you think I'm an idiot?

Sarah: No, Ann, you're a genius sometimes. But you do put things off.

Ann: I get them done.

Sarah: But at the last minute.

Ann: But you're so bossy. I mean — you're even controlling my
damn hair!

Sarah: You know how hard it is to get an appointment with Michael.
And you only like a perm after it's a month old.

Ann: Let me worry about it.

Sarah: But you'll be running around, phoning, begging for an
appointment.

Ann: Oh, I know, it's just that all this planning makes me tired. I feel
hemmed in. I can't move, can't think — you're always telling
me what to do.

Sarah: (Defensive)
If I don't, they don't get done.

Ann: Maybe they don't need to.

Sarah: Like your sweater. A perfect idea — a light warm sweater for
Greece. We rushed out to get the wool, I spent a whole week
showing you how to get started. Now where's the sweater?

Ann: Big deal. I picked too hard a pattern.

Sarah: It is a big deal. You're always doing it — starting things and not
finishing them.

Ann: Well, we'll finish this trip — we have the damn tickets —
thanks to you. But if I had known all the fuss it would have
caused — I'd never have committed myself. I wanted to go to
Japan anyway.

Sarah: Now she tells me. Why didn't you say so?

Ann: When? Eight years ago? When I was in the prenatal stage?
Would that have been soon enough?

(Ann is beside herself with frustration. Guilty, Sarah is quiet. She too
wishes she hadn't planned this trip with Ann.)

(Finally in Greece.)

Sarah: Where were you?

Ann: I found a whole street of antique stores. I lost track of time.
Then when I came out I had forgotten which direction the
hotel was in. I walked the wrong way for blocks. Finally I saw
that cafe where we had lunch and realized where I was. Sorry.

Sarah: Sorry? (Furious.) Sorry? We had tickets to the play — Sophocles
           — in Greece — a chance of a lifetime — and you're sorry.
Ann: We? — We had tickets? *You* bought them. Last week. You. Not
           we.
(Ann is equally outraged.)
(Both girls are confused, not sure of the source of all this anger.)
Ann: Well, I'm going out.
Sarah: (Icily) Please be so kind as to pick up some of your junk before
           you do. I can't find the sink it's so cluttered with cosmetics —
           and your sweaters are scattered everywhere.
Ann: Oh — do allow me to stack my lipsticks in alphabetic order —
           I can color-code my sweaters, piling them in a long straight
           row — never letting green get near red — . . . . (In tears) And
           by the way, I am going out to find my own room. Where I can
           relax for ten minutes. And maybe even go out for lunch to
           some place where I'd like to dine.
(She leaves slamming the door. Sarah, though upset, is strangely relieved.)

When "definitely" meets "I'm not sure yet" it
can mean trouble. Let's take a look. . . .

Sarah: I've always wanted to go to Greece.
Ann: There's so many places to choose
          from.
Sarah: Summer will be here before we know
          it.
Ann: I should get some brochures at the
          travel agency.

(One week later.)
Sarah: Did you get those brochures yet?
Ann: Sarah, it's only January.
Sarah: Only. Only. We have to book months
          in advance, Ann — You know that.
Ann: Ok. Ok. Don't get excited.

Sarah: I don't want it to turn out like our
          holiday to the Rockies.
Ann: It was wonderful!

Sarah: We had no hotel reservations. We had
          to spend two nights in the tent.
Ann: We got to see a whole herd of moun-
          tain goats.
Sarah: But we hadn't planned to sleep in a
          tent. We had planned to sleep in a
          luxury hotel. It was supposed to be a
          holiday.
Ann: It was a holiday.

Sarah already knows where she'd like to go for her long-awaited holiday. In order for her to go ahead with any planning and preparation it is essential that she have this feeling of having decided. Ann, on the other hand, needs more information before she can decide. Her attitude is to plan "in general" and make a final decision as late as possible. This is not because she is irresponsible, as Sarah is often inclined to suspect. Rather, it is because Ann prefers the perceiving function. In order for Ann to decide where to go, she wants to look at the alternatives. Unfortunately, Ann and Sarah have a different perception of time. This is especially true if Ann is an intuitive and Sarah a sensing type. Until a decision has been made, Sarah will be anxious. Ann will find such anxiety unreasonable. Moreover, she will feel pressured by Sarah's insistence. Both girls are using up energy in a negative way.

As this negative energy mounts, the girls start to bicker, remembering past experiences when similar incidents caused their different preferences to become apparent. Sarah, disliking the uncertainty involved in not having made reservations, remembers the difficulty caused by having to sleep in a tent. Ann, not being bothered by the uncertainty, easily forgets it and remembers the good things which happened as a result of the spontaneous adventure she en-

Sarah: *I just couldn't relax not knowing what would happen from one day to the next.*

Ann: *Some holiday — if every second has to be planned.*

joyed so much. It is not that both didn't have the same good and bad experiences. It is that their foci and therefore their memories will be different. Ann found the most pleasure in the trip to the Rockies because it was unplanned. Sarah found this fact to be so upsetting she could not enjoy the benefits involved.

Sarah: *Well, if we go to Greece — we HAVE to plan it — we won't just 'happen' to be carrying a tent in our purses, dearheart.*

Ann: *Quit saying Greece all the time as if we've decided.*

This time Sarah is not going to suffer the same discomfort — a trip abroad must be planned. It becomes, then, Ann's turn to be uncomfortable.

(Three months later.)

Ann: *Sarah, if you leave one more "list" for me I'll burn this apartment to the ground.*

Sarah: *Wow, aren't we in a good mood.*

Ann: *Well, it's bad enough at work — punch in, type this, file that, mail these, punch out, run for lunch, be at this meeting, meet this deadline, arrange for that flight, punch out, run for the bus.*

Ann's discomfort is augmented because she has a job not suited to her typology. Her job obviously demands a great deal of planning and scheduling. This drains energy from a perceiving type who is much more suited to a job allowing many degrees of freedom. A secretary's position is not such a job. Ann has been thinking of becoming a beauty consultant. It would be a good switch.

            My life is an alarm clock of agendas and I come home to "Ann, please make sure you have done the following:
1. Check passport
2. Arrange for shots
3. Order back pack
4. Write to Tony
5. Make appointment for perm"
God, Sarah, put in a dime, turn the crank. Back off. I'll be ready for this trip. Ease up — it's not even fun already.

Sarah: *(Offended, confused)*
        I'm only trying to help.

Ann: *Do you think I'm an idiot?*

Sarah: *No, Ann, you're a genius sometimes. But you do put things off.*

Irritated, fatigued from too tight a structure, Ann comes home to more imposed structure. She blows up.

Sarah does not understand. Her suggestions are sound. She recognizes Ann's frustration in getting things done at the last minute. She also knows that a little planning can avoid such frustration. Two things naturally motivate her — frustration and her ability to plan. She does not realize that Ann is not nearly as frustrated by hassle as Sarah herself is. Also she does not realize how hemmed in Ann feels by her "bossiness."

In fact, both girls feel a little guilty and therefore defensive at this point. Sarah knows she is too bossy, it's something she has been accused of many times before. Yet she can justify her actions — she almost feels it her duty to help Ann out. And her requests are not unreasonable. Ann knows that she leaves things until the last minute. It bugs her too. Also, she often starts projects that she leaves un-done for months or even abandons.

The great difference here is one of degree. Sarah needs closure. Ann does not. Although each girl may be upset by her own inability to use the least preferred organiza-tional pattern (in this case, Ann can't plan, Sarah can't "let it be"), it is the nature of people to behave childishly, unreasonably, when the weakness of their preference is pointed out. The reason for this is that the criticism implies that the inferior function must be used. The inferior func-tion is often an unreasonable im-mature character lurking some-where in all of us. If the girls were aware of the reasons behind their differences, they could be careful in how they both criticize or help one another. Instead they chal-lenge, blame, feel guilty, feel used. They steal one another's

Ann:	I get them done.
Sarah:	But at the last minute.
Ann:	But you're so bossy. I mean — you're even controlling my damn hair!
Sarah:	You know how hard it is to get an ap-pointment with Michael. And you on-ly like a perm after it's a month old.
Ann:	Let me worry about it.
Sarah:	But you'll be running around, phon-ing, begging for an appointment.
Ann:	Oh, I know, it's just that all this plan-ning makes me tired. I feel hemmed in. I can't move, can't think — you're always telling me what to do.
Sarah:	(Defensive) If I don't, they don't get done.
Ann:	Maybe they don't need to.
Sarah:	Like your sweater. A perfect idea — a light warm sweater for Greece. We rushed out to get the wool, I spent a whole week showing you how to get started. Now where's the sweater?
Ann:	Big deal. I picked too hard a pattern.
Sarah:	It is a big deal. You're always doing it — starting things and not finishing them.
Ann:	Well, we'll finish this trip — we have the damn tickets — thanks to you. But if I had known all the fuss it would have caused — I'd never have committed myself. I wanted to go to Japan anyway.

sense of freedom. Acknowledging their differences and coming to an agreement on which areas they can "give in" on could change the whole relationship. If Sarah needs some sense of control, the girls could agree to plan the essentials — purchase tickets, make reservations, arrange for a few specific tours. However, spontaneity could also be part of their plan — one week of "que cera, cera" to please Ann, perhaps a separation within the holiday proper. Ann could benefit from Sarah's planning abilities, letting Sarah "take care of business," thereby saving them BOTH energy. Sarah can, and often does, benefit from Ann's occasional inspirational finds — a hidden church, or quiet beach, an unusual shop, that perfect restaurant. Instead they quarrel. Ann feels trapped, resentful. Sarah feels fustrated, confused.

The feeling persists on their trip. True to her nature, Ann forgets herself in strange places. She becomes intrigued, loses track of time, gets lost, forgets commitments. She punishes Sarah, but it is not intentional.

Intentional or not, the hurt is real. But Sarah is not the only one hurting. Ann lashes out at Sarah's insistence on order. Judging types love things in their place, tidy, accessible. Perceiving types do not care. A holiday is a time to "let loose." What is already a chore at home is certainly not going to

Sarah: Now she tells me. Why didn't you say so?
Ann: When? Eight years ago? When I was in the prenatal stage? Would that have been soon enough?
(Ann is beside herself with frustration. Guilty, Sarah is quiet. She too wishes she hadn't planned this trip with Ann.)

(Finally in Greece.)
Sarah: Where were you?
Ann: I found a whole street of antique stores. I lost track of time. Then when I came out I had forgotten which direction the hotel was in. I walked the wrong way for blocks. Finally I saw that cafe where we had lunch and realized where I was. Sorry.
Sarah: Sorry? (Furious.) Sorry? We had tickets to the play — Sophocles — in Greece — a chance of a lifetime — and you're sorry.
Ann: We? — We had tickets? You bought them. Last week. You. Not we.
(Ann is equally outraged.)
(Both girls are confused, not sure of the source of all this anger.)
Ann: Well, I'm going out.
Sarah: (Icily) Please be so kind as to pick up some of your junk before you do. I can't find the sink it's so cluttered

*with cosmetics — and your sweaters
are scattered everywhere.*

Ann: *Oh — do allow me to stack my
lipsticks in alphabetic order — I can
color-code my sweaters, piling them
in a long straight row — never letting
green get near red — . . . . (In tears)
And by the way, I am going out to
find my own room. Where I can relax
for ten minutes. And maybe even go
out for lunch to some place where I'd
like to dine.*

*(She leaves slamming the door. Sarah, though
upset, is strangely relieved.)*

plague her vacation. Let the room stay messy — who cares?

Sarah does.

Consequently when Ann leaves, they both experience a sense of freedom and relief.

How Much Is Enough?

The initial step in improving communication is often a listening skill. I have suggested that passive listening is not enough. It is also essential to be able to see things from the other person's point of view. Psychological type provides a system with which to understand people's perceptions. It encourages empathy.

So is that it? I hear you. I understand. That's a good start, but. . . .

This "but" can be especially troublesome when one person lives with another person who is his opposite type. A person's opposite has a different focus of energy, perceives the world in a different way, makes decisions differently, and organizes the world in a different way. Moreover, one partner values most the very function which is least favored by his "opposite." This least favored or inferior function, being a person's weakest point, often causes annoyance to the person. Sensing, for example, is my inferior function. I have some pretty deep-rooted negative feelings concerning this area. Consequently, when I am trying to understand a sensing type's point of view, not only do I have to adjust my thinking to accommodate hers, I have to deal with some personal negative impulses of which I may be unaware.

One obvious solution to this dilemma is to become aware of the inferior function and to work on becoming more skillful in using it. This ability to use whatever function a situation demands is, according to Jung, the earmark of a mentally healthy, mature individual. Most of us naturally focus on this total type development in middle age. With awareness and training, it can begin earlier.

The more one considers differences among people's perceptions, the clearer it becomes that there are no absolutes. It is all a matter of degree. Awareness of others' points of view, acceptance of self, and development of inferior areas all help in this complex human process we call communication. Because our ability to communicate well is so fundamental to healthy, happy living, it deserves our attention, our energy.

Energy becomes a key point here. Instead of using our energies positively, we tend too often to squander feelings and time in a negative fashion. Much energy is lost in working against one another's preferences. To be forced into one's inferior preference takes a great deal of energy. To feel guilty about one's apparent "weakness" or deficiency steals energy. To misunderstand another's motives or actions and to be hurt by them gobbles even more energy.

Understanding of psychological type reduces this tragic waste. But understanding does not always come easily. Nor does experience. The tricky part is the whole issue of degree. It is extremely difficult to comprehend fully the degree to which our "opposite" type is different from us.

This lesson became startlingly clear one fall when I was asked by a Quaker community to give a workshop in communication skills, using psychological type. I was quite astonished by the number of intuitive, feeling, perceiving (NFP) types living in the community. It is inherent to the Quaker spirit that individual differences be respected and that, through sensitive exploration of alternatives, community decisions be made for the general good of everyone. This approach to life demands flexibility, compassion, creativity, and the community was comprised of many NFPs to inspire and execute good plans for such a life-style. But so does such a life-style need stick-to-itiveness and a fine working out of details. That task was often left to the one sensing, thinking, judging (STJ) male in the community.

When I met him he was frustrated. He was almost ready to leave the community. His wife looked worried and under stress. Tears filled her eyes as she spoke of some of the differences between her husband and herself. She, like most of the others, was her husband's opposite type.

The hours spent with this couple were very frustrating, and yet interesting and rewarding. The couple cared about one another very much. They had dedicated their lives to using communication and understanding to come to common decisions. Yet both felt they were being suffocated by the other's dominant functions.

The husband simply needed structure and closure. The wife could only function creatively when allowed to be spontaneous and flexible. She needed the freedom to abandon tasks (sometimes only for a period of time) if she felt others captured her interest. She postponed making decisions until she had collected all the information she felt she needed.

Carefully the couple listened to me as I explained their psychological preferences. Both agreed that their opposite preferences were the source of anxiety. I advised both to "give" as much as possible: she to finish tasks he cared about; he to allow her freedom, especially when he had little personal involvement in her projects.

"But I do!" they both cried. And they did. They were bending, giving, to the point of almost being ill. Yet the degree to which these two people were different made all that compromise appear to be non-existent.

Each had the same complaint. The loss of rights! He could not function when she abandoned projects he had put energy into. She fell apart by noon when each morning he left lists of tasks for her to complete.

We all recognized something that afternoon — the uniqueness of the human spirit. Our understanding, our appreciation, our respect grew. Astonished, slightly startled, we gazed at one another. We held one another in a silent moment of Quaker prayer. I had the feeling that if any people could resolve their differences these two could. And would.

The understanding of psychological type is clearly an important step towards improved communication. It is also clearly not a magic wand of instant mutual appreciation. It demands effort on the part of people working towards improved relationships. The greater the degree of difference in couples, the greater will be the effort required to insure each is accepting, is accommodating. It seems that an open or receptive attitude is initially required to truly permit the actual acceptance, the actual accommodation to take place in day-to-day living.

A "danger" inherent in the understanding of type became apparent to me this winter as I was supervising student teaching. Awareness of that danger may lessen the chance of trouble resulting. Often, opposite types are very conscious of, and irritated by, one another's different attitudes and perceptions. For example, a sensing judging-type teacher had become upset by an intuitive perceiving student teacher's seeming lack of planning. This discrepancy in degree of desired organization and control became clear during an after-school session. I explained to each the nature of their types and consequent differences. Because antagonism and uneasiness had already been established, neither the teacher nor the student teacher really heard the explanation. They heard only what they KNEW already — "He likes control." "She is unorganized." Instead of easing tension, I had succeeded only in reaffirming negative opinions already held by these two people. It is essential — when using an understanding of type to improve communication — that one be open to accepting the differences in others as being both natural and good. The weakness of one type is the strength of the other. The controlling type is also very stable, very reliable, very systematic. The unorganized type is very flexible, very creative, very open-minded. Both possess marvellous virtues. Being overly sensitive to the things that bug us about opposite types may blind us to their good points.

This "blind" spot and this "reaffirming of negative suspicions" does not confine itself to differences in function. An extraverted teacher complained to me that his introverted student teacher was too directive, she could not "let go." The observation was accurate. Introverted teachers do not work as well in spontaneous situations as do extraverts. Introverts need time to reflect before acting. The very nature of this need requires that the teacher "be in charge" of the situation.[1] The teacher could choose to see "the fault" and say, "Ah, I KNEW it," and reject the student teacher, or he could help her to plan a variety of strategies in making her class more student-centred. An introvert needs to learn how to "let go," to learn which aspects of the teaching and learning she must be in charge of for

---

1. Lawrence and DeNovellis noted that the classrooms of observed teachers who were introverts were significantly more teacher-centred and more structured by the instructional materials than were the classrooms of extraverts. The classrooms of introvert teachers also had a significantly higher incidence of organized activities in which pupils had no choice. See G. Lawrence and R. DeNovellis, 1974, p. 4.

her own security, and which she can turn over to her students. What is very nice about the introverted teacher is the calm, reflective, consistent atmosphere she so easily, naturally creates.

> For as we have many members in one body, and all members have not the same office; So we, being many, are one body . . . and every one members one of another.

> Having then gifts differing . . . whether prophecy, let us prophesy . . . Or ministry, let us wait on our ministering: or he that teacheth, on teaching; Or he that exhorteth on exhortation. . . .
> Romans 12: 4-8, as quoted in *Gifts Differing*, Isabel Briggs Myers.

The Thinking Type is skeptical

5/So What?

Seven Questions

Seven is a good handy figure in its way, picturesque, with a savour of the mythical; one might say that it is more filling to the spirit than a dull academic half-dozen.

Thomas Mann, The Magic Mountain

1. Who Am I?

This section of the book deals directly with analysing one's psychological preferences. If you have already read the first four chapters of *Insights*, you may have a pretty clear picture of your type preferences simply by identifying with various descriptors in the book. You may want to check out your perceptions. Here is a simple way to do that.

Determining Your Own Type Using the Instant Insight Inventory (I.I.I.)

For an estimation of your type preferences, examine the following patterns and choose one or the other. Sometimes you will feel you do both, or that your choice would depend upon the situation. This is to be expected. Remember that typology is a dynamic, changing aspect in your life. Maturation suggests you can move from one function to the other according to need. However, one is preferred, demands less energy, is more natural. Try to answer according to the way you act in an everyday situation. You may have trained yourself to be very organized in your job — but how are you on a holiday, for example? How does it feel BEST to be?

Do not deliberate too long over answers. Do not omit any questions. Try to answer according to the way you really are. That way is wonderful for you. An understanding of your psychological preferences will help you to use the way you are to best advantage. Stage one is recognition. Please, begin —

Instant Insight Inventory

Circle either A or B for each statement.

1. **A** I answer a question quickly, sometimes without thinking.   *or*   **1.** **B** I like to think about something before I offer an answer or an opinion.

2. **A** I use trial and error with confidence.   *or*   **2.** **B** I like to go deeply into understanding something before I try it.

3. **A** I need to find out what others expect of me.   *or*   **3.** **B** I like to do things on my own.

4. **A** I get full of energy when I am around a lot of people, such as at a party.   *or*   **4.** **B** I get tired when I am around a large group of people, and need to get away often to be by myself and collect my thoughts.

5. **A** I enjoy a lot of variety and action.   *or*   **5.** **B** I enjoy a quiet place all my own where I can reflect uninterrupted.

6. **A** I enjoy looking at details and proof that things are really as they appear to be.   *or*   **6.** **B** I tend to skim over details and look for hidden meanings in things.

7. **A** I enjoy checking, inspecting, reading the fine print, finding out all the information I can.   *or*   **7.** **B** I become impatient with routine and repetition and slow, precise activities.

8. A   I enjoy things as they are, recall past events, and learn from the combination of these two in a "common sense" sort of way.   *or*   8. B   In a flash of insight "I go with my hunches" on many things.

9. A   It would be fairly accurate to describe me as being realistic and practical.   *or*   9. B   It would be fairly accurate to describe me as being imaginative and inventive.

10. A   I rarely rely on inspiration to keep me going.   *or*   10. B   I have a lot of bursts of energy, with slack periods in between.

11. A   A need for justice rules much of what I do.   *or*   11. B   Harmony is one of the most important aspects of my life.

12. A   I try to analyse logically all the facts in making a decision.   *or*   12. B   I think of what is best for all the people involved in making a decision.

13. A   I consider fair and honest criticism to be a natural, acceptable part of human relationships.   *or*   13. B   I avoid confrontation and feel very uncomfortable giving or receiving criticism.

14. A   I know lots of people who are too soft-hearted and emotional in making decisions.   *or*   14. B   I have my feelings hurt by people who tend to analyse or make cold statements when understanding is what I am looking for.

15. A   I often have difficulty in freely expressing the emotions I am experiencing.   *or*   15. B   I find it easy to express my feelings and to understand the feelings of others.

16. A   I like to be in control of the events in my life and make them "the way they ought to be."   *or*   16. B   I need to understand thoroughly the events in my life and therefore spend more time than I should in making decisions.

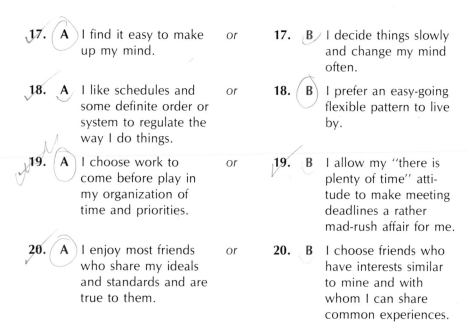

17. **(A)** I find it easy to make   *or*   **17.** **B** I decide things slowly
up my mind.   and change my mind
                                                 often.

18. **A** I like schedules and   *or*   **18.** **(B)** I prefer an easy-going
some definite order or   flexible pattern to live
system to regulate the   by.
way I do things.

19. **(A)** I choose work to   *or*   **19.** **B** I allow my "there is
come before play in   plenty of time" atti-
my organization of   tude to make meeting
time and priorities.   deadlines a rather
                                                mad-rush affair for me.

20. **(A)** I enjoy most friends   *or*   **20.** **B** I choose friends who
who share my ideals   have interests similar
and standards and are   to mine and with
true to them.   whom I can share
                                                common experiences.

To score your I.I.I. preferences, use the following guide:

Give yourself a score of one for each choice of A or B.

1.	A — extraversion	1. B — introversion
2.	A — extraversion	2. B — introversion
3.	A — extraversion	3. B — introversion
4.	A — extraversion	4. B — introversion
5.	A — extraversion	5. B — introversion

A score of 3, 4, or 5 As indicates a preference for EXTRAVERSION.
A score of 3, 4, or 5 Bs indicates a preference of INTROVERSION.

Give yourself a score of one for each choice of A or B.

6.	A — sensing	6. B — intuition
7.	A — sensing	7. B — intuition
8.	A — sensing	8. B — intuition
9.	A — sensing	9. B — intuition
10.	A — sensing	10. B — intuition

A score of 3, 4, or 5 As indicates a preference for the SENSING function.
A score of 3, 4, or 5 Bs indicates a preference for the function of
INTUITION.

Give yourself a score of one for each choice of A or B.

11.	A — thinking	11.	B — feeling
12.	A — thinking	12.	B — feeling
13.	A — thinking	13.	B — feeling
14.	A — thinking	14.	B — feeling
15.	A — thinking	15.	B — feeling

A score of 3, 4, or 5 As indicates a preference for the THINKING function.
A score of 3, 4, or 5 Bs indicates a preference for the FEELING function.

Give yourself a score of one for each choice of A or B.

16.	A — judging	16.	B — perceiving
17.	A — judging	17.	B — perceiving
18.	A — judging	18.	B — perceiving
19.	A — judging	19.	B — perceiving
20.	A — judging	20.	B — perceiving

A score of 3, 4, or 5 As indicates a preference for the JUDGING pattern.
A score of 3, 4, or 5 Bs indicates a preference for the PERCEIVING pattern.

Now that you have determined — your orientations: Extraverted (E) or Introverted (I)
— your functions: Sensing (S) or Intuition (N)
Thinking (T) or Feeling (F)
— your interface: Judging (J) or Perceiving (P), your overall type will begin to emerge, in a kind of skeletal form — ENTP, ISFP, and so on.

ENFJ

For a brief account of your type's overall characteristics, look up your "initials" and read the description under the corresponding letters on page 192.

If you are a bit uncertain as to which is your preferred type, look now at your least preferred or opposite type. If, for example, you think you are an ENFP, your total opposite will be ISTJ. The overall typology includes the preferred orientations (Extraversion or Introversion), the preferred functions, dominant and auxiliary (sensing or intuition, feeling or thinking) and a preferred interface (judging or feeling). The ENFP, then, has an extraverted orientation, a dominant intuitive function, an auxiliary feeling function, and a perceiving interface. This perceiving interface indicates that the ENFP prefers the process of perception to the process of judging. That makes the intuitive function the dominant, and the feeling function the auxiliary. The inferior function of the ENFP is the opposite of her dominant function. In this case that is the sensing function. The *overall* less preferred description, however, is opposite in every aspect of psychological type, that is, the ISTJ type. The description of the least favored way of behaving is found opposite dominant type descriptors on pages 192-193. The ISTJ is found to the left of the ENFP descriptor. E is always opposite I, S is opposite N, T is opposite F, and J is opposite P. The "opposite" of you in this context is sometimes called your shadow type. This shadow would describe what you are least like, the way in which you find it difficult and energy-consuming to function.

BRIEF DESCRIPTION OF THE SIXTEEN TYPES

ENTJ

Intuitive, innovative ORGANIZER; aggressive, analytic, systematic; more tuned to new ideas and possibilities than to people's feelings.

ESTJ

Fact-minded, practical ORGANIZER; aggressive, analytic, systematic; more interested in getting the job done than in people's feelings.

INTP

Inquisitive ANALYSER; reflective, independent, curious, more interested in organizing ideas than situations or people.

ISTP

Practical ANALYSER; values exactness, more interested in organizing data than situations or people; reflective, a cool and curious observer of life.

ISFP

Observant, loyal HELPER; reflective, realistic, empathetic, patient with details, gentle and retiring; shuns disagreement, enjoys the moment.

INFP

Imaginative, independent HELPER; reflective, inquisitive, empathetic, loyal to ideals; more interested in possibilities than practicalities.

ESFJ

Practical HARMONIZER and worker with people, sociable, orderly, opinioned; conscientious, realistic and well tuned to the here and now.

ENFJ

Imaginative HARMONIZER and worker with people, sociable, expressive, orderly, opinioned, conscientious, curious about new ideas and possibilities.

ESTP

REALISTIC ADAPTER in the
world of material things; good-
natured, tolerant, easy going;
oriented to practical, first-hand
experience; highly observant of
details of things.

ESFP

REALISTIC ADAPTER in human
relationships; friendly and easy
with people, highly observant of
their feelings and needs;
oriented to practical, first-hand
experience.

ISTJ

Analytical MANAGER OF FACTS
AND DETAILS; dependable,
decisive, painstaking and
systematic, concerned with
systems and organizations;
stable and observant.

ISFJ

Sympathetic MANAGER OF
FACTS AND DETAILS; concerned with peoples' welfare,
dependable, painstaking and
systematic, stable and
conservative.

INFJ

People oriented INNOVATOR of
ideas; serious, quietly forceful
and persevering; concerned
with the common good, with
helping others develop.

INTJ

Logical, critical, decisive IN-
NOVATOR of ideas, serious, intent, highly independent concerned with organization, determined and often stubborn.

ENFP

Warmly enthusiastic PLANNER
OF CHANGE; imaginative; individualistic; pursues inspiration
with impulsive energy, seeks to
understand and inspire others.

ENTP

Inventive, analytical PLANNER
OF CHANGE; enthusiastic and
independent; pursues inspiration
with impulsive energy, seeks to
understand and inspire others.

This is often a helpful strategy in finally choosing your pattern. If you say,
"that's me" when you read the descriptors of your type and can say,
"that is NOT me" of your opposite type, then probably you have ac-
curately determined your type from this short questionnaire. If you
disagree with the description, then the descriptors may not be right for
you. Psychological type is only a description of preferences, it is not the
self. You know yourself best and should trust your own judgment.

2. How Many Are Like Me?

There is no simple answer to this question. In very general terms, in Western society, extraverts outnumber introverts three to one; sensing types outnumber intuitive types four to one; 60 percent of females prefer the feeling function and 60 percent of males prefer the thinking function; there is an equal division between judging and perceiving types. (Bradway, 1964; Myers, 1962)

In 1975, Myers conducted a study of general American school populations. In an average classroom containing thirty-five students he found that there are six times as many extraverted sensing types as introverted intuitive types (Lawrence, 1979).

IS 7	IN 3
ES 18	EN 7

E — 70%
I — 30%

S — 70%
N — 30%

T — female 40%
    male 60%

F — male 40%
    female 60%

J — 50%
P — 50%

Because almost every aspect of society is represented in a cross-section of American schools, it may be safe to generalize that this represents the general population.

Most research has examined specific populations — schools, universities, job populations. In non-college groups, sensing types form 87 percent of the population. In academic groups, introverted intuitives far outnumber extraverted sensing types. Although all types enter most professions, some gravitate to certain professions more than to others. If you are in medicine, and are an IN, you will be like "most" people attracted to your profession. Teaching attracts "mostly" ESFJs; business attracts ESTJs; researchers are often NTs and writers are most often NFs. For more particulars on which types are attracted to specific careers, refer to question 6, "What Good Does Knowing This Do?" page 201.

3. How Can I Have My Type Tested?

You may, of course, wish to make do with the Instant Insight Inventory (I.I.I.), the quick survey of your preferences you made at the beginning of this chapter. Should you wish a more precise determination, however, you will find that the most widely used, readily available instrument designed for type testing is the Myers Briggs Type Indicator (MBTI), designed by Isabel Myers in 1962. The MBTI is a forced-answer questionnaire with a reliability of 0.85 tested by use of a logically-split-half procedure (Myers, 1962). It can be obtained and scored through several universities in Canada and the United States. The headquarters for the MBTI is the Center for the Application of Psychological Type, Suite B-400, 1441 N.W. Sixth Street, Gainesville, Florida, 32601.

Recently a new instrument, the Singer-Loomis Inventory of Personality (SLIP), has been developed at Wayne State University in Michigan (Singer and Loomis, 1980). Although not yet fully tested for reliability, SLIP has the advantage of transcending the bipolar opposites suggested in other inventories. It is the contention of the authors that opposite preferences do not necessarily (although they commonly do) exclude each other. Their inventory allows discrimination between those people who conform to the pattern of bipolar oppositions and those who deviate from it. Further research will allow more specific insight into SLIP's accuracy and usefulness.

In his book on type for teachers, *People Types & Tiger Stripes*, Gordon Lawrence has developed an inventory for determining personality type related to teaching and learning styles.

Keirsey, in *Please Understand Me*, has developed a similar inventory, the Keirsey Temperament Sorter, for self-determination of temperaments in type (as described in question 7 of this chapter).

Although there are several other instruments on the market, these are the ones I would recommend. For research purposes, or for a clearer certainty of type determination, the MBTI is presently the best. As a part of self-analysis and understanding, any of the self-determined questionnaires will be useful, as it is the process of answering the questions as much as the final scoring that leads to understanding of type preferences.

4. Can Type Explain What Motivates Me?

It seems it can. Certainly it can help.

An exploration of attitudes reveals that extraverts experience an *external* source of motivation which leads to a need to "check things out," whereas introverts enjoy an *internal* source of motivation which allows a very personal locus of evaluation.

ξΝ F?

In addition to this overall pattern, it has often been suggested that functions can affect motivation and become apparent as behavior patterns or temperaments. These "temperaments" can be traced back to the Greek Hippocrates. Keirsey[1] takes the notions of Hippocrates, includes the descriptions of type function as conceived by Jung, and presents four distinct personality blueprints. Each has a most unique motivational construct. None of the constructs have been scientifically researched, but they make for interesting speculation.

The first temperament membership is composed of the followers of the Greek god of the spirit, Apollo. These members share the intuitive feeling (NF) temperament. Guided by the spirit, this type is motivated by a desire to be true to the self. The NF is a man in constant search of his true self. His goal is always to have a goal. Needing to be unique, needing to be genuine, the NF searches endlessly in his quest for truth, for self-actualization. The key goal in the world of the NF is UNIQUE IDENTITY. Famous intuitive feeling types are Joan of Arc, Fritz Perls, and Isadore Duncan. A martyr, a revolutionary self-actualizer, and a promoter of free spirit, each contributes in a unique fashion, with missionary zeal, to a personal sense of truth.

The other intuitive type, the intuitive thinking (NT) temperament, is also in search of truth. But her quest is the seeking of truth in knowledge. For in knowledge lies power; not power over people, but power over nature. The natural scientist is an NT personality. Edison, for example, who chose to remain deaf so that he could isolate himself, is a good example of the NT pursuing knowledge even at the price of sacrificing personal interaction. In the true spirit of sacrifice and the pursuit of knowledge, Prometheus is the symbolic leader of the NTs. Prometheus, punished for bringing to man the gift of fire, a gift which empowered man over nature, was chained to a mountain. Each day a great vulture tore his liver from his aching flesh; each night the body restored itself.

Powerful is this motive of the NT to search, explain, make better. Driven by a compulsion to improve, the NT is extremely self-demanding, self-critical, and is often most successful in whatever she pursues. Yet, strangely, this type rarely appreciates her own achievements, always expecting a high level of performance and excellence.

Interestingly, the sensing perceiving (SP) personality — so different from the NT — is similar in the aspect of being driven. The SP is driven not to achieve, but to do — whatever he wishes, whenever he wishes. The goal, then, is freedom. Not freedom as an end, or a means to an end. There is, essentially, no END, no PURPOSE. There is only BEING. This most process-oriented type acts on impulse, not design. The motive, or goal, is

---

1. In Keirsey and Bates, *Please Understand Me*, 1978.

to have no goal. The king of whim and whimsey, the SP is a follower of
Dionysus, god of music, song, and dance, god of joy.

Great performing artists are often SPs. Elvin Presley and Bette Midler are
examples of SPs who sing, not to become great musicians, but to sing.
And by so doing, BECOME great. It is not the goal, simply a pleasant side
effect of the endless pursuit of doing, doing, and doing again.

The sensing judging (SJ) temperament, too, can be found doing, doing,
and doing again. Often, unfortunately the SJ is taking on all this activity
because she has to; not because she wants to. The SJ's life is full of "have
to's" and "shouldn'ts," for this type is guided by a sense of duty and
responsibility. Followers of the god Epimetheus, like their leader, they
would be duty-bound to stay with a wife such as Pandora, despite the fact
that she lets loose a thousand ills on mankind.

Sensible, responsible, conservative, the SJ can always be counted on,
trusted. Motivated by a need to serve, to nurture, to conserve, to govern,
this type is often found as a leader of an institution whose purpose is to
keep the status quo and to serve society. Say good morning to your local
police chief, school principal, bank manager, and you are probably
greeting an SJ personality.

5. Does Type Ever Change?

Jung never addressed the issue of type being a consequence of heredity,
environment, or a combination of the two. He described type as being
observable in very young children, and indeed this has shown itself to be
the case as recorded by such type watchers and researchers as Myers,
McCaulley, Keirsey, Lawrence, and Mamchur.

Research (McCaulley, 1977) has shown that for most individuals type re-
mains constant. You naturally have preferences that stay as favored
attitudes and processes for a lifetime.

In mid-life a process begins to occur which Jung called *individuation*.
This is the process of transcending the opposite attitudes and functions, of
bringing to fulfilment the collective qualities of the personality. This process of fulfilment, according to Jung, brings us closer to the total
archetypal personality of the "universal human being."

As part of that process, for example, the extravert may tend to behave
in introverted ways. Quiet, reflective time in a private territory may
become more a part of the extravert's life-style. This does not mean he rejects his previous preference for an outward-looking attitude towards the
world. He is STILL an extravert, he still feels comfortable in the extraverted attitude. But he ALSO can appreciate and experience the introverted attitude. His personality does not change, exactly — his

awareness is simply expanded and takes on new pleasures. This "newness" may give a *feeling* of change in type and is often wrongly interpreted as such. When a right-handed pianist learns to play expertly with the left hand, it does not mean she is no longer right-handed. Just let a flower vase threaten to spill on her grand piano and watch with which hand she automatically rescues it.

It should be noted, however, that when placed in a strange or threatening environment, an individual can lose confidence in his natural way of behaving. As a result, preferences are abandoned and the person either jumps uncomfortably from one function to another, truly trusting none, or may actually "change" type and cling desperately to his inferior function.

This reality became very clear to me when I functioned for one year as a teacher-therapist in a reform school. My prior working experience had been as a high school English teacher. In that setting I could be outgoing, trusting my environment (E). I could work on my hunches, "just knowing" how to teach (N). I used empathy, warmth, engaging my value system in all my decisions with my students (F), and the environment lent itself to easy, flexible planning in which I could relax and learn with my students (P). It was an experience filled with joy and confidence and for ten years my trust in my natural preferences grew. As a consequence, my functions grew stronger and more fully developed. I could move from feeling to intuition with ease. I had somehow achieved that lovely sense of having equal comfort with judgment and perception. What a rosy world. Why not try a real challenge? A "home" for hardcore delinquent girls.

Suddenly the values I had trusted all those years didn't work. I was warned by the administration that caring was dangerous. I was constantly conned by the girls, who cried in my sympathetic arms as they stole the keys from my unguarded pocket.

In the course of a year, my environment and the people in it became aggressive, hostile. I was surrounded by stabbings in the night, lesbian mothers visiting in the afternoon, stealing morning, noon, and night — pain, suffering, hopelessness.

Without warning, my hunches were all wrong. The things I tried failed. The things I didn't try failed.

I became my opposite psychological type. In reaction to what I considered to be a hostile environment, I retreated into myself (I). As my intuition failed, I tried to look for the facts, to face each moment realistically, one step at a time (S). As feeling failed me, I turned to the objective, the analytical, making decisions on logical analysis of the facts (T). At moments I would be so uncertain as to what was real (S) and what I should do (T), I belonged in neither perception nor judgment. I wavered back and forth, developing neither. In other words, I became a pretty shakey IST$_J^P$. It wasn't a very comfortable world. I lost 30 lbs., the ability to sleep, and my sense of humor. One year later I had quit my job, sold my house, and left the country. Two years later, I had regained my sense of humor, my teaching, and my natural ENFP type preference.

Often you can be hired *because of* your type (the reform school wanted a caring innovative enthusiast); but the job circumstances may make it impossible to function as you are. My best advice is to leave the job, find one suited to your personality, and return to the comfort and joy of developing your functions.

What I am saying essentially is that just as a parent or teacher may wrongly force a child to play a role not natural to him, so you may force yourself to play a role unnatural to yourself. Type may then appear to "change," but at a terrible price. The price seems to be worse and more lasting for the young. Neurosis and illness too often result. If, for example, a young man is instinctively, naturally, an introvert, but his parents force him into a extraverted role, he may "act" the part of the extravert. As a consequence, he rarely feels "right" with himself. He is forced into an attitude foreign to his nature. If he is an introverted feeling type, he may be forced to show emotions, to exhibit what would be most comfortably kept inside. The feelings may be "out there," but the introvert doesn't trust what's happening and loses a sense of reality.

Good type development demands, initially, a trust in the dominant function. The introverted feeling son, if allowed to keep his feelings to himself, to trust them as his INNER judgment function, will be confident in his decisions. He will be able to reflect on ideas, fantasize situations, bounce his values off each other, and feel a sense of peace. This frees the introvert to use his second favorite process, the auxiliary process, in the external or extraverted world. This auxiliary process may be sensation. The son will be observant, sensible, practical. The son will develop both a sense of perception and a sense of decision-making. This seems easier for the introvert than for the extravert (provided he is not FORCED to be what he is not). We all use the dominant process most frequently. However, as we have seen, it is the nature of the introvert to keep his favorite process for himself, for his inner world. He also uses the auxiliary or second-favorite process often, because that process is reserved for the external world. Because the introvert is forced to live in the environment and is forced to interact with it, most introverts get a lot of practice at both processes, the dominant and the auxiliary.

Extraverts, too, need this practice. Everyone has a favorite function — either perceiving (using the senses or the intuition) or judging (using thinking or feeling). Actually we use all four functions most of the time. Jung describes the functions as follows: ". . . sensation tells you that there is something. Thinking, roughly speaking, tells you what it is. Feeling tells you whether it is agreeable or not, to be accepted or not . . . and intuition (is) when a man has a hunch." (Evans, 1976, p. 100)

Although each of us uses all four functions, we all also favor one. That favorite is the dominant. If her dominant function is intuition, for example, the extraverted intuitive woman may be a marvel at "just knowing" many things — what's going to happen, how to do something, why someone did a certain thing. Her information system works well for her. However, she may have so much trouble making decisions, that it does her little good to "know" things. She may realize the stock market is going to fall, yet just can't decide to sell her shares. She may know how to write the essay, yet just can't organize herself into getting it done. She may know that Uncle Jake is angry because her husband drinks just one too many of Jake's beers, but she just can't decide if she should risk hurting her husband's feelings by telling him. The young woman suffers from an undeveloped judging function. She cannot make decisions. *Part* of the process is not good enough, even if that part works well. In order for the person to work very well — both perception and judgment must be developed.

This can happen quite naturally in the home or school. A child, a sensing feeling (ESF), for example, shows a good deal of common sense. Family members and class members trust this in the child. They ask the child's opinion regarding decision-making. If the child's dominant function is SENSING, he uses it to observe, to deal with the immediate issue. This observant, reliable quickness of perception feeds the child information. The information is used by the value system to form judgments. Thus the dominant perceiving function of sensing helps to develop the auxiliary or decision-making function of feeling. By encouraging and appreciating this process, by valuing the child's natural gifts, important others in the child's environment aid in this crucial process called total type development.

Once type development is achieved, individuation, the final stage of maturation, can occur, and the personality is able to tap the energy of each archetypal function. Both the conscious and the unconscious unfold. The individual uses sensation and intuition to realize a thing, uses thinking to analyse it, and uses feeling to evaluate it. There is greater choice, greater flexibility, greater efficiency.

On occasion I have tested students or clients and they appear on the MBTI to score "down the middle" on all categories — showing no preferences in orientation or function. In most cases, the person being tested has just experienced a deep trauma.[1] As a consequence, she trusts neither preference, and jumps from one to another. This is an uncomfortable and temporary position which usually "changes" as the trauma sub-

---

1. If you happened to score in the middle of the I.I.I., p. 245, do not be alarmed. There are three factors to be considered. First, the I.I.I. is only an estimate. It does not contain a wide variety of items as does the Myers Briggs Type Indicator (166 items). Second, it is common to have a split preference on one or another aspect of the typology. Many artists, for example, score as many preferences for the sensing function as the intuitive function. Third, the preferences are not static; they are dynamic. They move along the

sides and natural functioning can again dominate. This wavering back and forth can be described as an uncentredness. The person is unable to tune into what Jung terms the cosmic energy of the archetype because she cannot trust herself long enough to do so.

6. What Good Does Knowing This Do?

Self-Development

The most obvious and most important benefit of type knowledge is insight to the self. Bookstore and library shelves are filled with manuscripts on self-help. Too often they fail. It seems to me that the key to self-help is often understanding how or why we do what we do. Many self-help manuals prescribe precise measures of "how" without taking type into account. As a result many of these perfectly plausible schemes "go against" the type of many of the people trying them. The schemes end up being abandoned by those who often would most benefit from self-knowledge. What is worse, the person who tries an unsuitable scheme, and fails in using it successfully, may reinforce a negative self-image.

Typology suggests a way to understand and accept our whole self package, the strengths and corresponding weaknesses of our personality constructs.

Understanding of type helps to illuminate how we focus our energy, how we perceive, make judgments, and organize our environment. Within this knowledge lies the source of our dominant function, or strengths; and of our weakest or inferior function. The wise man, aware of his strengths, can make best use of them. That same man would also be wise to consider carefully the areas most likely to give him trouble. Instead of experiencing anger or fear, awareness allows for a calm acceptance and a chance to avoid or better prepare for situations which may cause difficulty. With this knowledge, even self-improvement programs that do violate our essential natures may be implemented.

Research (Myers, 1962) suggests that using the favorite or dominant function (your strength) leads to improved self-concept and academic achievement. It is simple common sense that if one knows what she does well, and does it often, she will feel good about herself and will come to

---

spectrum. I, for example, move between judgment (J) and perception (P), depending upon the circumstances I am in. Often when involved with a very perceiving, flexible person, I become more judging (J) to assure "the job gets done." If, on the other hand, my work partner is a definite J person who enjoys taking on responsibility, I slip happily into the P role of seeking alternatives, of being receptive and open to new ideas.

trust herself. That trust is contagious. It's like a great "success" bell ringing in the personality. She may learn, for example, that she is a feeling type and enjoys a fine capacity for being empathetic and caring. She trusts this and shows her caring at home, at work. People respond with appreciation and respect. Her success chime rings. That bell gets other bells bringing. Suddenly she can cook a more delicious supper, jog a more relaxed mile, type a neater letter, teach a more interesting lesson. She may also have learned in her study of typology that because she is naturally inclined to feeling, she is not so naturally inclined to making logical, analytical decisions. As her confidence in herself grows, so will her ability to cope with objective analysis. She may consult a friend or business associate who is good at it. She may hire an expert or accountant or lawyer. She may rely on herself, making lists of "pro" and "con," giving herself a few days "to think things over," or imagining what a scientist or business woman or principal might do if she were in her position. In other words, she would accept her weakness, and would calmly, without guilt or frustration or fear, accommodate for it.

We all "vaguely" know how we operate. Understanding of psychological type eradicates that vagueness. Hopefully, it also rings chimes of acceptance, success, and happiness.

Career Choice

A most logical follow-up of this awareness of strengths and weaknesses is to use typology in career counselling. The armed forces in the United States use the Myers Briggs Type Indicator to counsel their recruits in career selection within the forces. A Japanese version of the MBTI plays a key role in servicing the almost one million citizens using the Nippon Recruit Center situated in thirty-one Japanese cities. Because the idea of lifetime employment is widely accepted by Japan's people and its private companies, recruitment is concerned "not just with the abilities of prospective employees but with their personality, disposition, and character." (Oshawa, 1981, p. 1) Myers (McCaulley, 1977) conducted a fifty-year longitudinal study on the application of typology to medicine and other health professions. McCaulley conducted similar research involving engineering specifically (1976[d]) and various fields of science more generally (1976[b]).

McCaulley's research strategy for studying careers for types is:

1. *Interest:* Determine the types interested in the field. Which types are over- and under-selecting the field, in comparison to a base population?

2. *Selection:* Determine the types selected for training. Are some types over- or under-selected from the pool of interested applicants?

3. *Dropout:* Study the rates of graduation and dropout for each type.

4. *Practice:* Study practitioners. Are some types more likely to remain in practice, while others are more likely to leave the field?

5. *Specialty choice:* Study the types attracted to specialties within the field, and to different types of practice setting. Are specialties and settings more attractive to some types than to others?

6. *Satisfaction and competence:* How do the types differ in interest, motivation, method of work, competence, satisfaction, or frustration?

7. *Feedback to counselling:* Use what is learned from steps 1-6 to improve counselling. The goal is to counsel into careers the types showing high interest, low dropout, high career persistence, and high satisfaction and competence. Types with low interest, high dropout, low persistence, satisfaction and competence, can be alerted to these facts, and can be advised of fields where their type has found greater satisfaction and success.

(McCaulley, 1976c, p. 2)

The findings of such studies are very precise and helpful. Myers' 1977 study revealed, for example, that all types are attracted to medicine, but there are more INs than any other type. More specifically, extraverts are successful in surgery, pediatrics, physical medicine, and rehabilitation. Introverts prefer pathology, anesthesiology, psychiatry, and internal medicine. General practice and family medicine attracts the sensing types. The intuitive prefers the more specialized areas of psychiatry, neurology, cardiovascular diseases, teaching, and research. Thinking types gravitate towards pathology, feeling types towards pediatrics, judging types towards preventive medicine, and perceivers towards psychiatry, radiology, and administration. (McCaulley, 1977).

Studies of various professionals and college students (Keirsey, 1978; McCaulley, 1976b, 1976c) reveal that certain types are attracted to and succeed at certain jobs for a variety of reasons.

Extraverts enjoy jobs that offer high levels of interpersonal contact, rapid action, responsiveness to change, and opportunity to engage in pragmatic academics. Such professions as childhood education, business administration, and various practical practises in psychology have proven to be successful for the extravert.

Introverts seek jobs that provide sustained attention, a clear grasp of concepts, solitary work, one-to-one interaction, and research-oriented academics. They enjoy electrical engineering, art, zoology, philosophy, and forestry.

Folks preferring the sensing function enjoy jobs that lean towards care and precision, consistency in following established practices, skill in action rather than in words and symbols, practical work, attention to day-to-day events, use of well-learned knowledge, and jobs which are located in small communities. Childhood education, accounting, physical therapy, nursing, construction, and physical education are often recommended.

Those folks preferring the intuitive function seek jobs that reveal patterns in complex systems, use creativity and imagination to see possibilities, allow for the creation of new approaches, are intellectually challenging, and are located in the changing environments of larger cities. History, forestry, sociology, architecture, occupational therapy, psychology, chemistry, journalism, English, and art appeal to the intuitive.

Thinking types gravitate towards jobs that involve technical skill with equipment, knowledge of physical science, and tough-minded objectivity. Construction, political science, electrical engineering, and business are favorite professions.

Feeling types prefer jobs involving the human component, caring for and understanding people. Education, health-related occupations, English, sociology, and art appeal to the feeling type.

Judging types require jobs that provide schedules, systems, and order. Electrical engineering, accounting, nursing, veterinary medicine, physical therapy, engineering, and childhood education are professions filled by peoples preferring the judging function.

Perceiving types do best in situations requiring constant adaptability to changing demands. The professions which challenge this type are forestry, psychology, history, journalism, English, art, and occupational therapy.

Job preferences can also be analysed according to the motivational patterns of the Keirsey temperaments as described in question 4.

Can Type Explain What Motivates Me?

Intuitive types enjoy professions of psychiatry, clinical and counselling psychology, the ministry, teaching, missionary work, and the Peace Corps. Because they can speak and write fluently, often with poetic flair, many NFs enter communication media. Above all, NFs enjoy a sense of mission, and helping others becoming kinder, warmer, and more loving human beings. Occupations in which they can FIND THEMSELVES are most appealing. As a consequence of these preferences, NFs seek interaction and work towards perfection in a profession combining SERVICE and MISSION.

The Intuitive Thinker (NT) is above all a scientific type in search of control and understanding, prediction and explanation. Jobs which demand doing well under varying circumstances attract the NT. In these jobs he is relentless in his pursuit of high standards of competency. Whatever the work, it is important the NT choose carefully, for more than any other type, the NT lives in his work. That work is often concerned with bringing to bear some form of understanding — developing models, exploring ideas, and building systems. Careers in science, technology, philosophy, mathematics and logic, design and engineering, research and development, management, manufacturing, criminology, cardiology and securities analysis — all appeal to NTs.

Although NTs are often attracted to these scientific-oriented professions, we cannot assume that other types should not equally be valued in these professions. Clearly it is the nature of the NT to enjoy objectivity, to enjoy analysis, synthesis, specualation. It is also the nature of society to demand these attributes be present in their scientists. Of value, too, is the careful, objective, common-sense sensing type. A scientific research team in Washington was having difficulty in achieving results. The members seemed to be working independently of one another, in a variety of interesting but scattered areas. When a consultant analysed the team using the Myers Briggs Type Indicator, she found all five team members to be composed of Introverted Intuitive Thinking Perceiving types. As introverts they were great at thinking over ideas, but were not facile in exchanging those ideas, or even in trusting one another. As intuitive perceiving types they were brilliant at innovating, but rather reluctant to bring closure to their experiments, always yearning for more information, for further exploration. As thinking types they were adept at objective analysis. However, they lacked the skills necessary to insure good team communication and co-operation. An extraverted feeling type was sorely needed by this team to enhance the team spirit, to examine values, to resolve conflicts. A sensing judging type was required to observe and record, to bring some "common sense" to the scene, and to encourage closure on some projects. It was impossible to find an ESFJ scientist, though many applicants were available. Finally, an ENFJ and an ISTJ were hired. Within two months team progress improved. Moreover, the team members felt more unified as a team and more satisfied as individuals.

"Be Prepared" is the motto of the Sensing Judging (SJ) temperament, and prepared he will be for any job he chooses. The parental attitude predominating in the SJ personality forces him into jobs of service and responsibility. His job "home" is ultimately the INSTITUTION, which he loves to establish, nurture, and maintain. SJs will become teachers, ministers, accountants, librarians, bankers, clerks, nurses, barbers, security guards, insurance agents, managers, and salesmen. All these jobs possess a common denominator: the desire to conserve. The SJ with his sense of duty and his need to save, to conserve, and to maintain order and sensibility becomes the stabilizer of society. Many an industrious SJ is found as the leader, the administrator, the principal, the manager of his chosen "institution." Putting tremendous energy into maintaining the "good," the "right" in society; providing wonderful care for the young and old — these reveal the SJ involved in activities at his best — being loyal, honest, untiring, unselfish, dedicated.

The same sense of duty, power, spirit of sustenance is not found in the Sensing Perceiving (SP) type. Action is the key to this personality. But it is not the action of purpose or goal — it is the action of "free to be."

Impulsive, joyful, needing to be free of restraint and compulsion, the SP is charming and optimistic, and moreover, possesses an endurance level far beyond that enjoyed by any other type.

"Jobs" in the regular sense do not appeal to this type. The male SP seems to have the advantage, as more male-oriented careers offer opportunity for a combination of freedom and action. Mention truck drivers, the armed forces, troubleshooters in business, soldiers of fortune, racers, gunsmiths, surfers, cardsharps, and you automatically think of the male. The SP enjoys using tools, machinery, engaging in professions demanding precision, endurance, danger. Again the male comes to mind. Professional athletics; jobs involving heavy machinery; rescue squad, police and detective work; bartending, bellhopping, building — all SJ jobs, and all seldom occupied by women. That image is slowly changing, and the SP woman will appear more and more in the '80s as a woman of action and adventure.

Models, dancers, and singers are often SPs combining a natural talent and a love of action. Here women have shared equal opportunity with men. Professional performing attracts the SP who plays, or dances, or sings for endless hours — not to achieve an end, but for the immediate pleasure of playing, dancing, and singing. In this way this type, too, offers her special and wonderful gifts to the world.

Business

Just as typology affects career choice, so it affects how we behave in that career. If the career happens to be business, teaming becomes a key issue. Good teamwork demands a wise use of opposite types to supplement one another in a joint undertaking.

If group members are to work well together, they must be able to see one another's point of view. This is not always easy among opposite types.

Use of typology demands an initial understanding of what each type can contribute. Since what is one type's weakness is the opposite type's strength, each can benefit from one another's differing preferences. (See chart, "Mutual Usefulness of Opposite Types," page 207.)

Mutual Usefulness of Opposite Types

INTUITIVE NEEDS A SENSING TYPE:

To bring up pertinent facts
To apply experience to problems
To read the fine print in a contract
To notice what needs attention
   now
To have patience
To keep track of essential detail
To face difficulties with realism
To remind that the joys of the
   present are important

SENSING TYPE NEEDS AN INTUITIVE:

To bring up new possibilities
To supply ingenuity on problems
To read the signs of coming change
To see how to prepare for the
   future
To have enthusiasm
To watch for new essentials
To tackle difficulties with zest
To show that the joys of the future
   are worth working for

FEELING TYPE NEEDS A THINKER:

To analyse
To organize
To find the flaws in advance
To reform what needs reforming
To hold consistently to a policy
To weigh "the law and the evid-
   ence"
To fire people when necessary
To stand firm against opposition

THINKER NEEDS A FEELING TYPE:

To persuade
To conciliate
To forecast how others will feel
To arouse enthusiasm
To teach
To sell
To advertise
To appreciate the thinker

(Myers, 1974, p. 7)

By understanding differences in this complementary way, opposites can come to work together in not only a more efficient manner, but in a more mutually pleasing and satisfying manner.

Myers (1974) describes a superior management team she was asked to analyse. The team profile can be diagrammed as follows:

The top executive is an ESTJ, a typically efficient executive type; he will be practical, outgoing, thoughtful, objective, decisive. Four other members are TJ types. If their basic framework is similar, these types will form a strong team as they make decisions easily based on a logical analysis of the facts. The frequencies of the eight preferences in the group are:

4 extraverts
5 sensing types
6 thinking types
5 judging types

4 introverts
3 intuitive types
2 feeling types
3 perceptive types

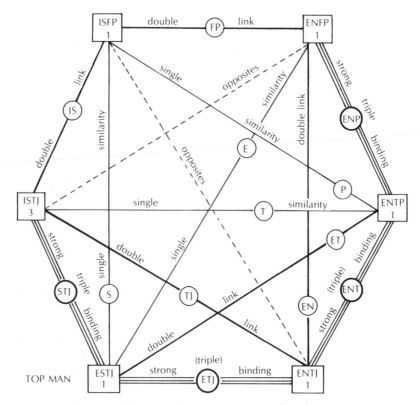

Types Found in a Superior Management Team in Industry

The top man has three preferences in common with at least four other team members. He also has something in common with EVERY member of the team. Communications will be good in this team. There are only two instances of complete opposite types. Although these types may have trouble communicating, there are several types who can bridge gaps between them.

This individual team is predominantly composed of thinking types, not unusual in such an operation. The helping professions (teaching, nursing, the ministry) attract more feeling types.

In this organization, the extraverted feeling type is in charge of industrial relations; again, a good matching of job and type.

An analysis of most "successful" operations will reveal similar matching. Knowledge of type has come to be widely used by industry in Canada, the U.S., and Japan to help organize industry. This is especially true in Japan where an individual often picks a single employer to last him for the entire span of his career. To date, almost one million people in Japan have been "typed" using the Myers Briggs Type Indicator (MBTI). (Oshawa, 1981)

North Americans may be wise to learn from these Asians so determined to unite the self and the environment. Understanding both makes better that union.

Marriage

If knowing your type can help you choose, or keep, or better enjoy a job, can it do the same for choosing a mate and enhancing a marriage? Frankly, as an intuitive feeling type my instinct tells me that love is love, and type can do little in "determining" a mate; however, it is most helpful when it comes to keeping and appreciating that loved one.

Differences in type between husband and wife may be a source of enjoyment, challenge, or friction. It is less likely to be the latter when the sources of the differences are clearly defined and understood. Chapter 4, "A Rose Is a Rose Is a Rose," is designed to clarify how understanding of psychological type improves communication in marriage.

According to psychiatrists who use typology in marriage counselling, the most common and most bitter conflict between types occurs between extraverted females and introverted males. The wife's wish for sociability runs counter to the husband's need for privacy and retreat from the external world of work and people. A second source of trouble occurs when the introvert needs reflection time and the extravert wants to discuss an issue immediately. Only by clearly understanding that the differing needs are real, are not being used as weapons, and can be accommodated through mutual agreement, can both partners feel uncompromised, understood, and cared for.

Finding mates with differing decision-making preferences is a frequent occurence simply because there are more feeling-type women than men. (60 percent of females are feeling types; 60 percent of males are thinking types.) The most common complaint among feeling types who marry thinking types is that their mates are too often cold, critical, and not expressive or responsive enough in matters of the heart. Perhaps it would be easier for mates to accept the different degree of expectation each has if they realized too that the faults or weak areas of a partner are probably only the reverse side of the partner's most admirable traits. That "cold" thinker is also a tower of strength in the midst of crisis and a wonderful ally when objective reasoning is called for.

"Understanding, appreciation, and respect make a lifelong marriage possible and good." (Myers, 1980, p. 131) If similarity in type leads to these three, it is wonderful. If similarity does not occur, understanding of the differences may well serve instead.

School

Understanding, appreciation, and respect constitute fine qualities for mutual sharing in the classroom as well as in the home. Often these terms are vague ideals towards which all teaching aspires but few class members actually, actively, and systematically achieve.

Psychological type provides a system whereby teachers can not only declare to students that they respect them enough to appreciate individual differences, but that they understand the differences and can adjust curricula in such a way as to accommodate those differences!

The teacher using typology has at his disposal the knowledge of how a student "catches on," learns, perceives, takes in information. This can occur through the senses or the intuition. Each way is remarkably different. Because most students in a typical classroom are extraverted sensing types (18 out of 35), one would think schools would be geared to this realistic, active, hands-on, appealing-to-the-senses type of learning, so necessary for and natural to the extraverted sensing type's learning style. And indeed, many great educators have advocated just such patterns.

> "Learning is active. It involves reaching out of the mind."
> (Dewey, 1977, p. 276)

> "In a pedagogical method which is experimental, the education of the senses must undoubtedly assume the greatest importance."
> (Montessori, 1964, p. 167)

Unfortunately, schools have been designed, by and large, by introverted intuitive types (university professors, writers of school materials, designers of curricula, members of the ministry, college teachers of teachers). These types learn best by reading, creative thinking, analysing, hypothesizing, seeking possibilities. They value such activities and consider them to be the marks of an intelligent and well-educated person.

And indeed they are. However, they are not the ONLY indicators of intelligence and learning. These attitudes influence not only what is taught and how it is taught, but how learning is evaluated and whether students are to be admitted to institutions of higher learning or continuing education.

> From 8th grade through graduate school, introverts with intuition tend to score highest on academic aptitude measures, and extraverts with sensing score lowest. The ranking of the quadrants is usually IN<EN<IS<ES.
> (McCaulley, 1976b, p. 5)

In 1967 Myers analysed the admissions policies and the drop-out rates for fifty-three diploma schools of nurses. She found that the types with the lowest drop-out rate are found, as would be expected, among the types most interested in nursing, that is, among the four FJ types. The surprising point is that the drop-out rate for SFJ types (who prefer sensing) is significantly *lower* than the drop-out rate of the NFJ types (who prefer intuition). This result is the exact opposite of what would be predicted from aptitude scores, because sensing types average about 7 points lower than intuitives on IQ and 50 points lower on the SAT (Standard Achievement Test). It must be concluded that the SFJ types have a specific aptitude for nursing that makes up, in most schools, for their disadvantages in scholastic aptitude.

Such being the case, an immediate attack upon the twin problems of recruitment and drop-out could be made by admitting more applicants who are ISFJ and ESFJ.

> These are plentiful types; they supply 38% of the class of 1967. They are strongly attracted to nursing. They succeed better with lower aptitude than other types. But because of their lower aptitude scores they may be undervalued by admissions committees. Ironically, an effort to improve a school's output of nurses usually involves raising the cut-off-point on admission test scores, thus excluding more and more of the SFJ types with their special vocation for nursing.
>
> (Myers, 1967, p. 1)

In this period of close scrutiny of testing practices, educators would be wise to examine all blindspots and biases that might be built into our system. Each type has a special gift to offer. Society would be foolish not to appreciate and develop every citizen so that each one of us can experience life at the highest degree of happiness and success possible.

Recognizing differences is a wise beginning. Not penalizing individuals for *being* individuals is equally important. The fullest use of type comes when teaching styles are developed and learning styles encouraged based upon an understanding of the different types. Gordon Lawrence has written *People Types and Tiger Stripes* (1979) to assist teachers in applying an understanding of psychological type to the classroom.

7. Can Type Preference Be Observed?

YES, but. . . .

Once understanding of the various preferences has been internalized, it becomes a natural process to "see" behavior in terms of type preference. The ability to do this obviously relates directly to the degree of comprehension the observer possesses.

The observed behaviors which indicate the various personality traits are outcomes of the interplays between orientation and functions and interface in individuals. Of these three aspects of type preference, orientation is the most significant factor for the observer to consider. This is because the nature of orientation indicates the person's main flow of interest, her major focus of attention.

Extraverts focus their attention on the outer world of the environment, of people and things. The environment is the favored, most comfortable, most natural, most trusted arena. For that reason extraverts *extravert*, or show, their dominant function.

Introverts prefer the inner, subjective world of ideas and relationships. They focus attention and interest, energy and trust inward, towards the private world of the self. This inner world, then, becomes the favorite, safest place in which to exercise the dominant function; the dominant function is kept for the self, or *introverted*, by introverts.

This factor of extraverting and introverting dominant functions becomes a crucial consideration in determining and observing psychological type. It is a fairly straightforward matter to observe the action-oriented and reflection-oriented behaviors in people. A very simple test is to ask the person a question. The extravert will immediately begin to answer; the introvert will pause and consider before answering. This reaction will occur in most cases.

As you spend more time with an individual you can ask yourself, "How much do I really KNOW about this person, about how he really thinks and feels, about his personal affairs and beliefs?" If he is an extravert, you will probably know quite a bit; if he is an introvert, you will have little personal data.

On the whole, an extravert is more relaxed, more at ease, more energetic in the environment. The introvert will appear to be more tense, often a little nervous and reserved. He may also be very introspective and insightful, but unless you know him well, this fact will not be obvious. To observe this aspect of the introvert's nature, you must choose a topic of deep interest to the introvert. Extraverts are often amazed at how thoughtful and perceptive the introvert really is — once they get to know him. This aspect of the introvert's personality must be coaxed to the surface. Often first impressions change when time is taken to really discover the introvert's true attitudes and perceptions. "Casual acquaintances think him (the introverted thinking type) inconsiderate and domineering. But the better one knows him, the more favourable one's judgment becomes, and his closest friends value his intimacy very highly." (Jung, 1971, p. 385)

Once the observer feels that orientation has been satisfactorily determined, the next aspect of typology to consider is interface. The behaviors which can be observed in a person preferring the judging interface are: having a clear sense of what "ought to be," organizing easily, being punctual, meeting deadlines, getting the job done. In a person preferring the perceiving interface, one might observe: the putting off of decision-making, avoidance of schedules, an easy, flexible attitude towards task completion, frequent requests for more information, a spontaneity.

The interface preference indicates the way in which the person deals with the environment, how the person *extraverts*. For the extravert, this will be with the dominant or favorite function: for the introvert, it will be with the second favorite, or auxiliary function.

> Jung has discovered that the primary function alone is extraverted in the extravert and introverted in the introvert, all three of the inferior functions taking the opposite attitude (or orientation) by way of compensation, which explains why nobody is every wholly extravert or wholly introvert.
>
> (Briggs, 1981, p. 9)

An extravert preferring the judging interface will have a judging dominant function, either thinking or feeling. An extravert preferring the perceiving interface will have a perceiving dominant function, either intuition or sensing. If the preferred judging function is dominant, the perceiving function will be auxiliary.

The opposite is true for the introvert. For this reason, observation often fails us. It is a simple matter to "see" the extravert use her favorite function of sensing, for example, because she uses it all the time. To determine the introvert's favorite function one cannot rely on observation alone. Here the interface must be carefully considered. The introvert preferring the judging interface shows the world her auxiliary function, thinking or feeling. The true favorite, reserved for the inner world, will be one of the perceiving functions, sensing or intuition.

Likewise, the introvert interfacing with the perceiving preference will deal with the world using sensing or intuition; but the dominant function of introverted perceiving personalities is actually thinking or feeling. It is essential to remember that the introvert's actions portray the auxiliary and unless we delve deeper, we will miss the introvert at her very best.

Once orientation, interface, and thereby the possibilities for dominant and auxiliary functions have been determined, further observation will indicate which functions are actually preferred. Sensing will show up as a love of detail, of common sense, of being *observant*; intuition appears as a love of the original, of the implied, of being *expectant*. A simple test of preferred perceptive function is to question the person about what he likes to read. Sensing types will read books on facts, on "how to do," fishing magazines, books of lists, biographies, movie magazines, cookbooks. Intuitives love novels, poetry, books of theory, history, philosophy. You may further enquire concerning things they remember about what they have read, or seen, or done. Sensing types give great lists of details. Intuitives give impressions; they talk about style, symbol, hidden meanings.

The feeling function causes the person to be sensitive and tactful, valuing harmonious emotional relationships. This is a subjective, *personal* way of behaving. The thinking function arouses actions involving a logical, *analytical*, scientific attitude. The thinker will be prone to showing a strong reasoning power and a love for truth. Very simply, you can ask a person the reason behind a recent decision. The thinker will begin to give reasons for his actions. The reasons may include values and feelings, but they will be presented in a logical, analytical way. The feeler will immediately begin to relate how he felt it was the "right" thing to do, how others would be affected by his actions, how he just "had" to. It is more difficult actually to express this decision-making process for the feeling type. He does not find it difficult to express feelings, and emotions; but he finds it difficult to express the how and why of his feeling decision-making. The opposite is true for the thinking type. The answer for this lies in the nature of the process: thinkers can analyse the process because the function itself calls for analysis. "We become good by doing good; we develop a characteristic structure through habitual performance." (Von Franz and Hillman, 1979, p. 75)

It is natural, then, for the thinking type to be able to analyse his thinking process. It is more difficult for the feeling type to do so, for the feeling process is not analytical. There may be another reason, postulated by Hillman, namely, that the collective repression of the affective side of the psyche in our history leaves us with a sense of loss concerning feelings. "We are at a loss, not knowing how to feel, where to feel, why to feel, or even if we feel. There is loss of individual feeling style and form, as if an ability has got crippled." (Von Franz and Hillman, p. 75) Consequently, even the feeling type, who so naturally uses the function, may feel at a loss to describe how he uses it exactly. This is particularly true of the introverted feeling type who has a more reserved and inaccessible personality, valuing above all else the inner emotional life for its own sake.

This developmental view of functions shows the functions to be part of the development of the conscious personality, "forming part of the ego, its consistency, its habits, unity and memory, its characteristic way of performing." (p. 75)

It becomes clear that it is never enough to examine the aspects of psychological type in isolation. The observer must consider the whole personality, and the interactions between all four preferences. An extraverted, sensing, feeling, perceiving (ESFP) type and an introverted, sensing, feeling, judging (ISFJ) type share a similar dominant function (sensing) and auxiliary function (feeling). But because the extravert shows his dominant, you will observe the ESFP being very observant and practical. The behavior patterns most clearly shown by the ISFJ who introverts his sensing function will be the intensity and the tactfulness of the auxiliary function, feeling.

Moreover, the interplay between the sensing function and the interface so affects the motivation of the two types that they may often appear as "opposites," despite their similar function preference.

The sensing, perceiving (SP) personality is relatively goal-less, being a very free and easy, fun-loving, flexible, process-oriented being who cherishes the freedom "to do" above all things (see Question 4, "Can Type Explain What Motivates Me?" page 195). When the SP finds that thing she loves to do, she may dedicate herself to doing it with a passion that astonishes everyone around her. It is often said of such personalities, "they have found their niche."

The sensing, judging (SJ) personality is, in contrast, the most goal-oriented type, being a well organized, responsible, duty-bound, product-oriented being who accepts with determination whatever "niche" the world presents to him (see page 205).

It might be wise, at this point, to add a word about observing the inferior function. It is that function which sneaks up on us when we least expect it. Often the inferior function, being a sore spot, can be charged with emotion. If you notice a close friend or relative, anyone you know well, acting "out of character," it may be this inferior function you are seeing. Being the dark side of the personality, it may expose itself in the form of infantile or tyrannical behavior. A person acting in her inferior function can also appear defensive, vulnerable, insecure. "I did not forget such a simple thing!" insists the intuitive when reminded of an oversight. A few minutes later, this same person, easily influenced by others in matters involving the sensing function, asks, "Please show me the details *you* think are the most important."

The inferior function need not always reveal itself in the form of awkward or tyrannical or insecure behavior. Sometimes an ecstatic state is triggered by the inferior function. This stage, and the memory of it, can be so powerful that the person experiencing the so seldom used function may consider it to be a favored function experience. Remembering my delirious joy at the touch of silk, the smell of grass, the warmth of my baby's body next to mine, I was convinced when I first learned about psychological type that I was a sensing type. Close acquaintances, understanding these matters and me, only smiled. The person herself may be fooled by the inferior function; the truly knowledgeable observer is not.

To summarize, type can be observed by first examining all the pieces, then putting them together, observing interactions between the components. Key words, specific actions, general patterns of behavior will gradually become a part of the observer's perceptual field. Type watching becomes as natural as noticing various other relationships between people. "Those two are newlyweds — look how they are so shy and attentive to one another."

"Look at those brothers, they must be twins, they are dressed exactly alike. Not identical twins, though — see the shape of the nose. And the eyes are different colors."

But be careful. "That woman must be fond of her son." You have it all figured out. You have been watching the mother and her son. They look alike, both blonde, fair, tall, slim. He is so polite, so courteous, so caring. She looks at him with frank motherly pride. She tells you of his latest successes with a rock band. He blushes, puts his arm around her waist, "I couldn't have done it without your support, your encouragement." You secretly wish your son was that appreciative of all the support you've given him. You're so busy thinking these thoughts you almost miss the young man adding, "You're the best little wife a fellow could have."

So it is with psychological type. For years I assumed that a teacher and close friend was an introverted feeling type. I based the assumption first on the observation of his reflective nature in answering questions. He would always pause and consider. An introvert, wouldn't you think? And he was warm and caring, expressed many ideas and decisions in terms of feeling and values when we worked together. A feeling type, right?

Wrong. It was a good guess. It took a longer relationship, closer observation, and many talks with him, in fact, for me to be convinced that he was an extraverted thinking type. The pausing was his thinking function, objectively standing back to observe and analyse data before making a decision. As an extravert (and a person well versed in psychological type) he cared about people — in this case, me — and about the relationship. He used the language of feelings and values when working with me because he knew it was my preference.

It seems to me that the more mature and the more sophisticated the person, the less "safe" one can be in making judgments about type on observation alone. Often a frank discussion yields important information which must also be considered. In young people, where psychological maturity has not developed to the point of allowing so much choice in behavior, and where the person acts more spontaneously, according to natural preferences, it is easier to type by observation alone. However, it must be emphasized that whether one is observing the behavior of adults or children, typing cannot be taken too far. It explains only orientation, perception, decision-making, and interfacing preferences. It does not explain the whole personality. It becomes a matter of degree. Used in moderation, for the purposes intended (family counselling, career-choice, teaching/learning styles, effective teaming), it is an invaluable aid.

Because understanding typology is so helpful in the classroom, and because MBTI scoring for all students is often too expensive or time-consuming, I have developed an observation instrument to determine extraversion and introversion preferences in students (Mamchur, 1978). (See Appendix, page 223.) These preferences were chosen because they are the most easily observed and because they are so important to, but often neglected in, curriculum design.

The instrument and the accompanying manual is included as an appendix for the reader's examination. Those wishing to use it on a large-scale basis may obtain the requisite copies from CAPT, Suite B-400, 1441 NW 6th Street, Gainesville, FLA 32601.

The instrument was designed and tested for reliability as a low-inference observation tool. Low inference means that the observer does not evaluate but merely records on a score sheet behaviors he does or does not see. No judgments are necessary. Behaviors are described on the score sheets in a specific rather than a global manner. The descriptions stick as close to the actual behavior as is possible.

The importance of the low-inference design of the instrument lies in that it does not require the observer to have knowledge of type preferences to use it. If a person is beginning to understand psychological type, but feels a little hesitant in relying on that comprehension to determine type preferences, it is useful to use an instrument that does not demand expert knowledge. The process of using the instrument seems to serve as a training device to give the observer a sense of type watching. This procedure of looking at behaviors from another's point of view has been demonstrated (Combs & Soper, 1963) as a method of developing empathy.

Thus, using the observation instrument not only gives useful information, but offers the observer an increased knowledge of psychological type and a more empathic attitude towards people.

6/in... The End, It's Up to You

Imagine a scene, any scene. Imagine yourself in it. . . .

> Your boyfriend is late again. He stopped on the way to your house to buy some peaches. Peaches led him to examining the whole fruit section, on to the fish stand, followed by flowers, fresh and irresistible. He turns up one hour too late for roast, rare, and the bunch of daisies he plops into a jar doesn't appease a furious you. You can't tolerate how inconsiderate he is.

OR CAN YOU? . . . What can be done when a Judging preference bangs heads with a Perceiving preference?

> Your secretary has become nervous, edgy, of late. She is making mistakes she doesn't usually make. An efficiency expert has recently rearranged the office, moving your secretary from her old dingy desk stuck in the corner, away from everyone, to a more central location. Now she can keep an eye on everything that is going on, and she has a much cheerier, more sociable environment to work in. So what could be wrong? Is it the sudden change? Is she unfriendly?

IS SHE? . . . What happens when an Introvert is placed in an active environment where there is a lot of distracting stimuli?

> You and your husband are playing four hand at the piano. Whenever he makes a mistake you ignore it, partly because you want to spare his feelings and partly because you want to get on with the pure pleasure of the music. However, your husband, far more serious about the "practice," automatically clucks his tongue in disapproval every time you miss a note. God, how insensitive he is!

OR IS HE? . . . Does a thinking type's "perfectionist" nature have to steal from a couple's pleasure?

You are telling a story about the time you drove your family across Canada. Right in the middle of the exciting account of how you almost smashed headlong into a Safeway truck in Winnipeg, your daughter interrupts. She informs everyone that the truck was a Brinks, carrying money, not groceries, and furthermore, it was in Calgary, not Winnipeg. Your story is ruined, the mood gone, and you wonder why your daughter needs to be so picky. She must be in a bad mood.

OR IS SHE? . . . What happens when an Intuitive confuses facts and a Sensing type feels compelled to correct them?

With an understanding of psychological type comes a challenge, an opportunity, a responsibility. With an understanding comes more choice in how one might respond to a given situation, a given person. The response can be less defensive and more accepting, more adaptive and tolerant. The response, based on a knowledge of differences, with mutual understanding and open communication, can grow into an acceptance and appreciation of those differences. It's up to you.

Image a situation. Any situation. Imagine you in it.

You have just moved into the city and house buying is on your mind. You have your eye on a perfect little place, it has a large music room, a sunny porch, and a kitchen that would even delight your mother. In fact, the whole place reminds you so much of the home you grew up in, you have fallen in love with it. . . . You might be wise to consult with a Thinking type friend who will logically analyse all the factors involved in purchasing a home: price, value, short- and long-term investment, potential mortgage rates, suitability of size and location for your family, and for future resale potential.

Feeling types can benefit from the objective and logical council of Thinking types, particularly when important decisions must be made.

> You have again been invited by the local school board to teach a
> night class in family law. It is in your nature to be flexible and spon-
> taneous, not caring much for schedules or deadlines. But you know,
> from last year's experience, that quite a few of the folks taking your
> class were uncomfortable with your seeming lack of organization. This
> year you draw up a tentative schedule and distribute it on the first day
> of class, explaining to your students that areas of focus and time lines
> may change as need and interest dictate. To open each session you
> write the evening's agenda on the board. This frees you to be adap-
> tive, yet gives your class a sense of direction.

Those types preferring the perceiving function would be wise to accommodate the more structured "judging" types participating in group
situations.

> You are considering a job change, have worked on your own for a
> long time and you sure aren't getting rich. You have been offered a
> position as mechanic with a large manufacturing firm at a very good
> wage.
>
> Before you accept you might want to ask yourself a few personal
> questions:
> — How would I feel if I had to share a workspace?
> — How would I react if someone else finished a job I started?
> — How would I feel if I had no opportunity to suggest changes in the
>   way the plant operated?

Looking at personal preferences is essential in considering job choices.
Different types place priority on very different issues. Introverted Intuitives,
for example, prefer to be in charge of their own environments.

> Keen about understanding yourself, you purchase a book on
> psychological types. You are fascinated while you are reading, but
> within a month you have almost forgotten the ideas that so excited
> you. Your friend borrows the book and pretty soon you are discussing
> it, sharing and examining interpretations. You suggest you analyse the
> members of your family, the people you work with. "No," she says,
> "I think I'll read about it a bit more." She goes to the library and
> takes out *Psychological Type* by Carl Jung. You decide to enroll in a
> Saturday psychology course.

Different types prefer to learn in very different ways. Extraverts prefer a
group orientation, in which verbal interaction and practical application is
prominent. Introverts prefer a more reflective, individual approach,
carefully considering ideas before making a major commitment. Knowing
your learning style preference enables you to be a more successful independent learner.

Whether the situation involves the resolution of conflict, group leadership, job placement, or planning a personal learning strategy, an understanding of type can be more accommodating. Choices can broaden, decisions take into account strengths and weaknesses, varying needs, and different approaches. The long-range consequences of using type knowledge wisely can be a healthier, happier, more contented lifestyle. It's often, after all, up to you.

Appendix: AORO

An Observation Instrument to Determine Action-Oriented, Reflection-Oriented Preferences

Teacher's Manual for Use of AORO

The instrument (AORO) is a systematic observation instrument. That means that you record what you see. It is not necessary to evaluate what you record. The items on AORO describe behaviors you may observe as being action- or reflection-oriented. Each item was designed to be as low-inference as possible. That is to say, the descriptions of behavior are as precise and non-evaluative as the behavior will allow. However, some inference on your part will be necessary. You will have to be familiar enough with the students, for example, to differentiate between a depressed action-oriented child and an excited reflection-oriented child.

The actual process of using the instrument will help you to learn more about your students and how they are really functioning. AORO is designed to help the teacher develop a new frame of reference for observing and understanding students. This frame of reference will make it possible for you to plan curriculum around specific learning preferences. You can better group students, manage time and space and materials for working areas, and organize activities. Just when you use AORO is not too important. Use it as early as you feel comfortable with it. Remember your purposes are threefold:

1. You are learning a valuable frame of reference for yourself.
2. You are acquiring knowledge about your students that will aid you in curriculum planning.
3. You are gathering data on the students which can be recorded in their cumulative records to assist the teachers with whom they will work in years to come.

The instrument can be scored in the manner you feel it best for you to manage. It is a demanding task to teach and to observe simultaneously. For that reason the instrument is flexible — with no time requirements and no set number of students to be observed. It does not matter how many individuals you decide to observe and score. As familiarity with instrument and students increases, so will ease and efficiency of observation.

To facilitate the process of observing, a teacher could:

● observe one student per period and check off observations during the break; observe and score several students as another teacher (art, music, P.Ed., team) carries the major teaching responsibility;
● observe several students each day, checking off observations during any available moments;
● observe several students while they are busy at different assigned tasks;
● inform the students that the teacher is busy learning about them and needs time to fill in some papers each day.

Results could be shared with the children. Middle school students easily understand the concepts of their type; there is no evaluative connotation of good or better or smarter involved, and students come even more to appreciate the concern and expertise of their teacher. Moreover, awareness of the way the student tunes into the world is very helpful to the young person in understanding why some tasks are particularly difficult or annoying for her, and others are so pleasantly easy.

It is a natural tendency to see someone behaving one way in one situation, and assume, often erroneously, that person will behave that way again. It is also natural to remember one incident in which, for example, a student was very active and boisterous, and assume the child is action-oriented. *To avoid this natural danger in using an observation instrument it is essential that you check only the behavior you actually observe each observation period. Check each behavior only once each time you observe. It is not necessary to record the number of times the behavior occurs, nor is it expected that you will observe every item each observation period.*

Every child will display some characteristics in each category. This is normal. Scores will indicate the preferred way of tuning into the world. To score AORO simply add up the checks. "Mildly Evident" receives a score of one. "Very Evident" receives a score of two. "Not Evident" receives a score of 0. The category with the highest score determines the student's preference.

Because situations often influence behavior, it is a good idea to record the situation (math lesson, field trip, independent study) under which the student is being observed. It is best to observe each student at least FIVE TIMES before you make a final decision as to whether action or reflection orientation is truly the student's preferred pattern of learning.

In order for it to be possible to observe the students' preferred patterns of learning, it is essential that you observe during a period when the students have some degree of CHOICE in what they do. If students are functioning in a very closely structured setting, you may be observing teacher preferences rather than student preferences. It is natural, too, for teachers to tune into and to organize the world in the way that is preferred by them. The ideal is to have a classroom operating in such a way that all members of the group function at their optimal levels of efficiency. Awareness of these optimal levels helps to make it all possible.

AORO
Action Oriented

Student's Name _____ Teacher's Name _____

Present Situation _____

I. Prefers to act, then to think — learns by doing

Not Evident	Midly Evident	Very Evident	Do you see the student . . .
	✓		1. acting quickly
	✓		2. moving from object to object or from person to person
		✓	3. being impatient with delay
	✓		4. showing interest in activities involving doing something
	✓		5. choosing to use trial and error
✓			6. having a short attention span
	✓		7. showing impatience with long, slow jobs
✓			8. expressing a need to experience something in order to understand it
✓			9. sometimes taking on too many activities.

II. Prefers to work with other people — learns by interacting

Not Evident	Mildly Evident	Very Evident	Do you see the student . . .
	✓		10. choosing to work with others
		✓	11. asking what other people are doing
		✓	12. talking frequently with teacher
			13. asking how others solve problems
			14. eagerly attending to interruptions
	✓		15. readily offering opinions
	✓		16. talking over new ideas with other people
		✓	17. appearing friendly and congenial

III. Prefers to work orally — learns by talking

Not Evident	Mildly Evident	Very Evident	Do you see the student . . .
✓			18. being outspoken
		✓	19. being talkative
		✓	20. communicating well
		✓	21. being good at greeting people
	✓		22. adding new ideas when talking about an issue
✓			23. volunteering to talk in front of the class.

IV. Prefers an external source of motivation — likes to check things out with others

Not Evident	Mildly Evident	Very Evident	Do you see the student . . .
	✓		24. asking teacher for feedback on tasks being performed
	✓		25. asking questions to check out group expectations
	✓		26. choosing topics or assignments that have value to other people
		✓	27. expressing satisfaction over pleasing others
		✓	28. sharing personal experiences

Reflection Oriented

Student's Name _____ Teacher's Name _____

Present Situation _____

I. Prefers to think, then to act — learns by taking time to reflect

Not Evident	Mildly Evident	Very Evident	Do you see the student . . .
√			1. appearing to be deep in thought
√			2. taking time to think before acting
	√		3. holding back from new experiences
	√		4. pausing before answering
		√	5. being uncomfortable with spontaneous questioning
			6. searching for facts to confirm ideas
		√	7. asking questions to allow understanding something before attempting to do it
		√	8. sticking to complicated tasks
	√		9. having a long attention span

II. Prefers to work alone — learns on her own

Not Evident	Mildly Evident	Very Evident	Do you see the student . . .
			10. choosing to work alone or with one person
√			11. asking for a quiet space to work
√			12. showing annoyance at being interrupted
√			13. carefully selecting a few friends
√			14. appearing shy

III. Prefers non-oral learning — does his best work in his head

Not Evident	Mildly Evident	Very Evident	Do you see the student . . .
✓			15. being quiet
✓			16. enjoying library projects
✓			17. entering carefully and slowly into discussions
✓			18. having problems communicating orally
	✓		19. enjoying reading assignments
	✓		20. performing better in written work than in oral presentations

IV. Prefers her own internal source of motivation — likes to do things her own way

Not Evident	Mildly Evident	Very Evident	Do you see the student . . .
	✓		21. working intently on task at hand
	✓		22. working on one thing for a long time
✓			23. making own decisions
	✓		24. becoming frustrated when things cannot be done the way pupil feels they should be done
✓			25. setting own standards when possible
✓			26. seeming hard to understand
✓			27. being willing to pursue something independently without group or teacher approval
✓			28. being reluctant to give personal information

References

Ashton-Warner, S. *I passed this way*. New York: Alfred Knopf, 1979.
———. *Myself*. New York: Simon & Schuster, 1967.
Bradway, K. "Jung's psychological types." *Journal of Analytical Psychology*. Vol. 9. 1964, pp. 129-35.
Briggs, K. "Meet yourself: How to use the personality paint box." *MBTI News*, no. 1, Vol. 4, Fall, 1981, pp. 1-9.
Combs, A., and Soper, D. "The relationship of child perception to achievement and behavior in the early school years." Cooperative Research Project, No. 814, 1963.
Dewey, J. *Experience and education*. New York: MacMillan Publ., 1938.
———. *The middle works 1899-1924*. Vol. 2. Illinois: S. Illinois University Press, 1977.
Evans, R. *Jung on elementary psychology*. New York: E. P. Dutton & Co., 1976.
Folklore of the MBTI 1981. A collection of anecdotal stories available from Association for Psychological Type, Gainesville, Florida, 1981.
Godden, R. *Gone: A Thread of Stories*. New York: The Viking Press, 1968.
Jung, C. *Memories, dreams, reflections*. New York: Vintage Books, 1965.
———. *Psychological types*. Princeton, N.J.: Princeton University Press, 1971.
Keirsey, D., and Bates, M. *Please understand me*. Del Mar, California: Prometheus Nemesis Books, 1978.
D. H. Lawrence. London: Octopus Books, 1960.
Lawrence, G. *People types & tiger stripes*. Gainesville, Florida: Center for Applications of Psychological Type (CAPT), 1979.
Lawrence, G., and DeNovellis, R. "Correlation of teacher personality variables (Myers-Briggs) and classroom observation data." Paper presented at the annual meeting of the American Educational Research Association, University of Florida, 1974.
Loomis, M., and Singer, J. "Testing the bipolar assumption in Jung's typology." *The Society of Analytical Psychology*, 1980, pp. 351-56.
Mailer, N. *The executioner's song*. New York: Warner Books, 1979.

Mamchur, C. "Development of a systematic observation instrument for measuring action-oriented or reflection-orientation as preferred learning patterns of children." Doctoral dissertation, University of Florida, 1978.

McCaulley, M. "The Myers-Briggs Type Indicator and the teaching — learning process." A paper presented at the 1974 American Educational Research Association, available from Gainesville, Florida: CAPT, 1976 (a).

_____. "Personality variables: Model profiles that characterize various fields of science." Paper presented at the 1976 Annual Meeting of the American Association for the Advancement of Science, available from Gainesville, Florida, CAPT, 1976 (b).

_____. "Psychological types and career preferences." Action paper available from Gainesville, Florida: CAPT, 1976 (c).

_____. "Psychological types in engineering: Implications for teaching." Engineering Education, Vol. 6. No. 7, April, 1976, pp. 729-36 (d).

_____. The Myers longitudinal medical study, Monograph 11. Gainesville, Florida: CAPT, 1977.

Midler, B. A view from a broad. New York: Simon and Schuster, 1980.

Miller, A. An enemy of the people. Dallas, Pennsylvania: Penguin Books, 1951.

Montessori, M. The Montessori method. New York: Schocken Books, 1964.

Myers, I. The Myers-Briggs Type Indicator. Palo Alto, California: Consulting Psychologists Press, 1962.

_____. "Type and teamwork." A research report available from Gainesville, Florida: CAPT, 1974.

_____. "Relation of psychological type to drop-out in nursing." A preliminary research report available from Gainesville, Florida: CAPT, 1976.

_____. "Gifts differing. Palo Alto: Consulting Psychologists Press, 1980.

Neilson, W., and Hill, C., eds. The complete plays and poems of William Shakespeare. Cambridge, Massachusetts: The Riverside Press, 1942.

Nijinski, R., ed. The diary of Vaslav Nijinsky. Los Angeles: University of California Press, 1968.

Oshawa, T. "In Praise of Isabel Briggs Myers." MBTI News, No. 2, Vol. 3. Spring, 1981, p. 1.

Porter, K. A. The collected stories of Katherine Anne Porter. New York: Harcourt, Brace & World, 1965.

Robbins, T. Still life with woodpecker. New York: Bantam Books, 1980.

Russell, B. Autobiography. London: Unwin Paperbacks, 1975.

Thomas, A. Latakia. Vancouver: Talonbooks, 1979.

Thomas, D. The doctor and the devils. London: J. M. Dent & Sons Ltd., 1953.

Von Franz, M., and Hillman, J. Jung's typology. Irving, Texas: Spring Publications Inc., 1979.

Williams, T. The rose tattoo. New York: Signet Books, 1956.